Devon Recipes

Devon Recipes

Catherine Rothwell

AMBERLEY

To Barbara – My Best Friend

First published 2012

Amberley Publishing
The Hill, Stroud
Gloucestershire, GL5 4EP

www.amberleybooks.com

British Library Cataloguing in Publication Data.
A catalogue record for this book is available from the British Library.

ISBN 978 1 4456 0335 3

Typesetting and Origination by Amberley Publishing.
Printed in Great Britain

Contents

Acknowledgements   9
Author's Note   10
Conversion Guides   11
Introduction   15

Soups
    Summer Vegetable Soup   17
    Pheasant Soup   17
    Bideford Tripe Soup   18
    Bideford Carrot Soup   19
    Horrabridge Sheep's Head Soup   20
    Plymouth Cucumber Cream Soup   21
    Exmouth Devon Broth   21
    Sidmouth Good Wife Soup   22
    Exeter Spinach Soup   23
    Sidbury Vegetable Marrow Soup   24

Fish
    Appledore Salmon Pie   25
    Barnstaple Fish Stock   26
    Dartmouth Stewed Trout   27
    Killerton Smoked Haddock with Poached Egg   28
    Torbay Mussels   28
    Baked Brown Trout   29
    Baked Teign Trout   29
    Salmon Tail in Cream   30
    Brixham Sole in Cider   30
    Turbot in Cider   32
    Bream with Egg Sauce   32
    Red Gurnard with Sauce   32
    Bolt Head Marinated Herrings or Pilchards   33
    Babbacombe Devonshire Pasty   34
    Shortcrust Pastry   34

Kingswear Potted Buttered Crab meat   *35*
Laver Pickle   *36*
Saltwater Eels   *37*
Baked Turbot   *38*
Tiverton Salmagundi   *39*

Meat and Savoury Dishes
Roman Pie   *40*
Appledore Parsnip Cakes   *40*
Dartmouth and Okehampton Devon Sausage   *41*
Paignton Stewed Ox Kidney   *42*
Parsnips in Dripping   *43*
How to Tenderise Cheaper Cuts of Beef   *44*
Roast Partridge in Sherry Sauce   *44*
Ilfracombe Celery Stuffing   *45*
Chestnut Stuffing   *46*
Ilfracombe Redcurrant Sauce for Roast Lamb   *46*
Paignton Scalloped Mushrooms   *47*
Cheese and Bacon Scones   *48*
Tiverton Meat Loaf   *50*
Greenway Ham and Mushroom Omelette   *52*
Plymouth Lamb and Chestnuts   *53*
Plymouth Potato and Cheese Cakes   *54*
Ladram Bay Chestnut Savoury   *54*
Exeter Stew   *55*
To Prepare Rice for Curry   *56*
Exmouth Toad in the Hole   *57*
Dawlish Warren Jugged Hare with Redcurrant Jelly   *58*
Princetown Hog's Pudding   *59*
Roast Duck and Chestnuts – A Favourite at Devon Hotels   *60*
Okehampton Roast Beef and Gherkins and Suet Pudding   *60*
Tavistock Pheasant with Apple Sauce   *61*
Stoke Gabriel Lamb Stew   *62*
Exmouth Summer Herb Tart   *62*
Killerton Pork Hot Pot   *63*
Chicken and Leek Cobbler   *64*
Tavistock Beef with Dumplings   *65*
Devon Roast Lamb   *66*
Clovelly Meat Pasty   *67*
Lynton Herb Pasty   *69*
Exeter Early Summer Hotch Potch   *70*

Sandy Bay, Combe Martin Rabbit with Cream 71
Sidmouth Devonshire Brawn 72
Dartmouth Pie 73
Haunch of Venison 75
Bristol Mamble Lamb Pipkin 76
Brixham Tomato Relish 77
Apple Chutney 77
Apple and Sultana Chutney 77

Cakes, Puddings, Pies

Totnes Blackberry and Apple Flummery 78
Fig Flapjack 79
Wholemeal Cottage Loaves 79
Ginger Snaps 81
Appledore Apple Amber 81
Westward Ho! Coffee Marshmallow Whip 82
West Country Tart 83
Bideford Fruit Flapjacks 84
Devon Flaky Pastry 84
Teignmouth Honey Cake 85
Shaldon Apple Pie and Clotted Cream (also found at Sidmouth) 87
Salcombe Regis Cheese Scones 88
Date and Rice Pudding 88
Paignton Carrot Cake 89
Arlington Court Snow Pancakes 90
Torquay Caramel Peaches 92
Torquay Tipsy Trifle 93
Chudleigh Custard Pudding 95
Devonshire Splits 96
Okehampton Raspberry Tartlets 96
Lee Apple Scone 98
Sidmouth Apple Pudding 98
Salcombe Devonshire Junket 99
Damson Jam 100
Ashburton Victoria Sandwich 101
Old-fashioned Ashburton Raspberry Jam 101
Barnstaple Chocolate Soufflé 102
Stoke Abbott Steamed Raspberry Pudding 103
Dawlish Warren Devon Cream Biscuits 103
Lee Moor Gooseberry and Banana Pudding 104
Widdecombe-in-the-Moor Strawberry Pie 104

Widdecombe Fairings 104
Woolacombe and Lustleigh Shortbread 105
Totnes Chocolate Cake 106
Buckfast Honey Muesli 107
Cockington Date and Walnut Loaf 108
Crediton Pan Cake 110
Clovelly Gooseberry Pudding 110
Devonshire Clotted Cream 111

Devon Drinks, Jam and Toffee

Oddicombe Toffee Apples 112
Woolacombe Barley Water 112
Treacle Posset 113
Widdecombe-in-the-Moor Rose-hip Purée 113
Rose-hip Jelly 114
Hedgerow Wine 114
Lynmouth Blackcurrant Fool 115
Gooseberry Fool 117
Treacle Toffee Caramel 117
Treacle Toffee 117
Butterscotch 118
Torbay Mint and Apple Chutney (Pound Chutney) 118
Axminster Blackberry Wine 119
Axminster Raspberry Wine 119
Spiced Ale 120
Frumenty 121
Devon Cream Toffee 122
Buckfastleigh Chocolate Brandy 122
Chudleigh Coconut Candy 123
Ilfracombe Hazelnut Butter 123
Cherry Fruit Sauce 123
Apricot Sauce 124
Okehampton Rough Cider 124
Toffy 125
Kingsbridge Apple and Blackberry Jam 125
Kingsbridge Rowan Jelly 126
Dawlish Gooseberry and Elderflower Cream 126
Rockford Tomato Chutney 127
Babbacombe Greengage Fool 128

Acknowledgements

I would like to thank the following people and organisations for their assistance in the writing of this book: Barnstaple Library, Barnstaple Record Office, Glenys Battams, Bideford Library, Shirley Booker, Evelyn Boyd, the late Stanley Butterworth, Clovelly Village Centre, Dartmoor National Park, Devon County Library, Captain Enthovens, Exmoor National Park Information Centre, North Devon, The Exmoor Visitor, Joyce Gooding, Michael and Anne Gornall, Eric Hayes, Maurice Hanssen, M. Humphries, Mary Hobbs, Nichola Johns, Angela Lewin, Michelle Luke, Patricia Macarthy, Adam McElroy, Eve Martin, Mid Devon Tourist Association, The National Trust, North Devon Farm Park, North Devon Museum, Carol Nott, Margaret Price, Janet and Richard Pelling, Valerie Rook, C. W. L Salmon (of J. W. Salmon Ltd, Sevenoaks), David Skip, Sonnenheim Hotel, Bideford, Jack Stasiak, David Taylor, Mr S. R. A. Taylor, Tors Hotel, Lynmouth, the Tourist Information centres at Barnstaple, Bideford, Ilfracombe, Lynmouth, South Molton, Torquay.

To all others whose names went unrecorded, our sincere thanks for being so kind and co-operative.

Author's Note

Most of the recipes in this book are designed to serve four people, unless otherwise stated. Eggs are medium size. Imperial and metric measures are included – use one or the other, but do not mix them. Oven temperatures and cooking times are intended as a guide. If using a fan oven, reduce temperatures by 20 degrees Fahrenheit.

Conversion Guides

Oven Temperatures

	°C	°F	Gas Mark
Very Cool	110	225	¼
	120	250	½
Cool	140	275	1
	150	300	2
Moderate	160	325	3
	180	350	4
Moderately Hot	190	375	5
	200	400	6
Hot	220	425	7
	230	450	8
Very Hot	240	475	9

Imperial Weights and Measures (with Recommended Metric Equivalents)

Ounces	Grams	Ounces	Grams
1	25	9	250
2	50	10	275
3	75	11	300
4	110	12	350
5	150	13	375
6	175	14	400
7	200	15	425
8	225	16	450

Pints	Fluid Ounces	Millilitres
¼	5	150
½	10	300
¾	15	450
1	20	600
1½	30	900
1¾	35	1,000 (1 litre)

1 cup flour = 4 oz = 110 g
1 cup sugar = 6 oz = 175 g
1 cup butter = 8 oz = 225 g

Table of Equivalent Measures and Weights

1 breakfast cup	½ pints
1 teacupful	¼ pints
3 tablespoonfuls	½ teacupful / ⅛ pint
1 teacupful flour or chopped suet	¼ lb
1 small teacupful sugar	¼ lb
1 teacupful butter	¼ lb
1 teacupful breadcrumbs	2 oz
1 tablespoonful golden syrup	2 oz
1 heaped tablespoonful flour or chopped suet	1 oz
1 level tablespoonful sugar	1 oz
1 level tablespoonful butter	1 oz
1 dessertspoonful	½ tablespoonful
1 Quart	2 pints
1 Gill	5 fl. oz

Introduction

I often wish that I had clear
For life, 600 pounds a year,
A handsome house to lodge a friend,
A river at my garden's end ...

Whenever we come to Devon, beautiful country of fulfilled promise and pleasant surprise, setting aside that now absurd figure of £600, Jonathan Swift's sentiments in 1727 are mine today. Abounding in the brimming rivers, there are many such desirable places as the Dean longed for; indeed we stayed at one on the last night of our 1989 visit: 20 acres' shooting; high-walled garden; ice house; terrace; pheasants strutting in the long driveway and thick woods, at the end of which raced the River Mole. In the eighteenth century it had all belonged to a rich woollen merchant, with a mill at his garden's end, a man so prosperous he could commission Adam work and have executed true Devon, Ipplepaine marble columns for his handsome house.

Devonshire is dear to the hearts of many, each having his or her own idea of the country's essence in a nutshell. Sir Walter Raleigh rated it 'the county of red earth, ruddy apples, rosy cheeks and honest men'. Equally appreciative, lesser mortals have thought of a land of cream and roses, colour-washed houses, purple buddleia and pink hydrangeas, but all would surely agree on its variety. Unique in English counties, having two coastlines, a close second in size to Yorkshire, its rich diversity grew on us day by day as we journeyed: wide expanses of moorland with thickly wooded coombes furrowing to the ocean; village clusters of thatched cottages with a wealth of fourteenth- and fifteenth-century churches; ancient buildings; manor houses; parks; farms; tumuli; cliffs; sandy and shingly beaches; inlets where myrtles and geraniums still bloomed. We were savouring Devon in the quiet of early autumn, a discovery in itself. Although we remember long-stay holidays when our children were young, uninterrupted by motor cars, we now revelled in winding miles of high-hedged lanes washed clean and sparkling by the rains of the previous night.

We were in search of recipes inseparable from history and tradition. As one hotel proprietor said, 'You have come to the right place.' Devonians, after a seemingly endless season, had time to talk. A circle of Armada cannon in the open air at Bideford made history seem tangible. Barnstaple furnished five ships that joined Sir Francis Drake's fleet at Plymouth to defeat the Spanish, all sailing from the Great Quay in 1588. With such an abundance of coaching inns: the Cherub at Dartmouth; the fourteenth-century Rising Sun at Lynmouth, or the Mill Inn, 'last pub for miles', it was easy to conjure up scenes from 200 years ago, when bowls of hot punch or mulled wine, with handy ladles, were set in readiness for the coachmen who, although provided with a bear or tiger skin to throw over their knees, arrived in winter almost frozen stiff.

'Shark wreck and mackerel fishing' at Lynmouth, as a notice, may have been unique. The feat of its lifeboatmen between Thursday and Friday of 12 and 13 January 1899 surely was. This rescue of the crew of the *Forrest Hall*, crippled off Porlock, involved eighteen horses hauling lifeboat *Louisa II* up Countisbury Hill and over Exmoor. Launching at Lynmouth not being possible, they made for Porlock Weir, en route having to demolish a cottager's wall, and at Ashton Gate put the lifeboat on skids. Ten and a half hours later on Friday the 13th, at 6.30 a.m. the *Louisa II* was launched, reaching the wreck one hour later. Supermen! But this astounding story was followed by another two days later on our tour. Not all that long ago, Devon men feared to work outside without a dog to ward off the pixies!

The isolation of the Moor (for no true Devonian calls it Dartmoor) is awe-inspiring. Still a weird and dangerous place for the unwary, no wheeled vehicles could penetrate a century ago. Only travellers and pack horses made their way along the tracks between bogs marked by granite crosses and relics from man's earliest civilisations. Westmans's Wood is a remnant of ancient oak forest, 1,000 years old. On the Moor, Stannary Law prevailed, the tin miners of stanners of Ashburton, Chagford, Plympton and Tavistock holding their own Parliament in the open air at Crockern Tor. I delighted in villages where time is measured by the seasons, whose quaint names (some of which appear on no maps) include Martinhoe, Woody Bay, Kittitoe, Beccott, Snapper, but I missed the more dainty, rich-red cows of my childhood days, all of which seem to have been substituted by hulking black-and-white cattle. Sadly, we never saw a badger trundling along by the roadside, only dead ones knocked down by cars. To see the real Devon you have to leave your car and trudge over Dartmoor or along the lanes between the 10-foot-high hedges, some 8 feet across, alive with many species of bird, insect, plant and mammal.

To discover the real Devonian you have to talk about food. Response was as rich and varied as the coloured county itself. Many types and ages were generous, imparting the information we sought. We had indeed come to the right place.

Catherine Rothwell

Soups

The beaching of the cargo ship *Napoli* caused much trouble for the village of Branscombe, but the enterprising Vale Brewery thereupon invented a special ale to mark the happening. The brewery operates from a converted barn and Napoli's On the Rocks is a drink much enjoyed by locals and visitors to wash down with a Summer Vegetable Soup.

Summer Vegetable Soup

METHOD
The squash halves should be loosely wrapped in foil and placed on a baking sheet with the red peppers. Roast for 40 minutes at oven temperature 200° C. Then add the garlic cloves wrapped in foil. Take the skin off the peppers and remove any seeds. Chop up the flesh and join it with the flesh of the squash. Put into a pan with the stock and black pepper. The onion needs to be softened by 10 minutes boiling. Bring to the boil then simmer a little longer before liquidising the soup and adding plenty of chopped chives.

INGREDIENTS

1 squash, halved and seeds removed
2 red peppers
1 onion, well chopped
1 chilli, well chopped
4 cloves of garlic
Freshly ground black pepper
1½ pints vegetable stock
Chopped chives

Pheasant Soup

METHOD
Place the prepared pheasant in a stewpot and cover with the cold water. Bring to the boil, then reduce heat, simmering steadily for 1¼ hours. Add the vegetables, seasoning, bay leaf and spice. Keep the bird well covered with liquid and simmer on for a further hour. Remove the flesh from the bones of the pheasant. Strain the soup. The meat can be liquidised, but we preferred not to do so. Add the cream. Heat up very gently and adjust seasoning. Serve with sippets (small squares of dried toast fried in dripping) and watercress on side plates.

INGREDIENTS

1 pheasant
3 pints water
2 leeks
2 sliced carrots
1 celery heart
1 teaspoon mixed spice
1 bay leaf
Seasoning
¼ pint thick cream
Chopped parsley
2 medium onions, chopped

Bideford Tripe Soup

METHOD

Wash the tripe well and cut into small pieces. Peel and chop the onions finely. The parsnip should be washed, scraped and chopped. Cut the bacon small also. With the seasoning put all these into a big stew pan with the milk and water. Bring to boiling point and skim, then simmer slowly for 1½ hours. Mix the flour and water to a thin paste and add to the soup, which should never at any point in the long simmering boil fast. Stir for 5 minutes until the soup thickens, then it can be served.

INGREDIENTS

½ lb tripe
1 parsnip
1 pint milk
1 lb Spanish onions
1 rasher fatty bacon
1 pint water
1 dessertspoon wholemeal flour

The clapper bridge at Postbridge, Dartmoor, photographed by A. Judges Ltd, is a study of a centuries-old structure amidst the wild, desolate scenery of the Moor. Once they were to be found all over England, simple yet ingenious bridges helping postmen, packhorse trains, travellers, all and sundry. Basically, they were long, flat stones supported by heaps of small, flat stones doing service as piers.

Bideford Carrot Soup

METHOD

Melt the butter and fry the vegetables for 5 minutes. Add water, milk, rice, nutmeg and seasoning. Bring to the boil. Cover and simmer gently for 35 minutes. Stir in the lemon juice, then the cream.

INGREDIENTS

1 oz butter
8 oz grated carrots
1 medium onion, grated
1 pint water
1 pint milk
1 oz rice
A pinch of nutmeg
2 teaspoons lemon juice
3 tablespoons fresh single Devon cream
Ground sea salt and black pepper

Bideford was once one of the busiest ports in England, with ships trading to the West Indies and Spain. Bideford's twenty-four-arch bridge has spanned the River Torridge since the Middle Ages so it has been widened and strengthened many times. It also has an annual Regatta. Bideford also favoured traditional Good Wife Soup.

A hundred years ago this was reckoned a cheap, strengthening soup for people recovering from illness. Edward Capern was the postman poet of Bideford. After his death in 1894 the bell that he carried on his rounds was placed in a niche on his tombstone at Heanton Punchardon.

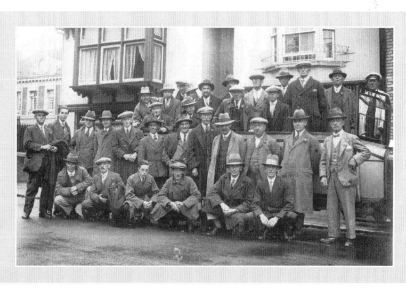

A men's Friendly Society arriving at Puddicombe on its annual Charabanc trip, 1920.

Horrabridge Sheep's Head Soup

METHOD

The head should be washed very well and left to soak in warm, boiled water for an hour. Remove brains and tongue. Put the head in a large pan with the bunch of herbs, the vegetables all cleaned and chopped, a teaspoon of coarse salt and a sprinkling of black pepper. Add 3 pints of water and bring to the boil. Skim and simmer steadily with the fine oatmeal for 2 hours. Meanwhile, wash the brains, removing any fibre, and boil gently in slightly salted water for 15 minutes. Pound them, mixing with butter and a few breadcrumbs. Stir this into the soup and simmer on for 1½ hours. Remove the meat from the head and put back into the soup, which will now be ready to serve. The tongue can be cooked along with the head, then skinned, to be used as a separate dish.

INGREDIENTS

1 sheep's head
Bunch of fresh herbs
1 small piece celery
A few stalks of parsley
1 tablespoon fine oatmeal
1 teaspoon vinegar
3 pints watercress
1 carrot
1 turnip
1 large Spanish onion
1 oz butter
2 teaspoons pre-soaked barley
seasoning

An 'oven-house lane' in the North Devon country denoted a public oven where you get bread and meat baked.

Horrabridge village is between Tavistock and Plymouth. The date is 1900 when the chief source of employment was provided by Horrabridge Brick Works. The bridge where the three girls and small boy are standing has its brick wall made from local clay. Jugged hare or rabbit with cream could have been part of the day's fare for these charming-looking children. Sheep's head soup, as well.

Plymouth Cucumber Cream Soup

METHOD

Wash and cut unpeeled cucumber in half lengthwise and scrape out seeds. Wash and scrape the carrot. Dice the vegetables and cucumber and snip the chives into small pieces. Boil the stock and put in carrot and cucumber. Boil for 10 minutes and add peas and chives. When the vegetables are tender pour the soup into a basin. Melt the butter in the same saucepan, stir in flour and gradually add the soup. Stir until it boils and boil for 5 minutes. Season with the salt, pepper and nutmeg. Remove soup from the heat and when it has cooled a little add the cream. Stir well and pour into a tureen.

INGREDIENTS

1 cucumber
12 chives
2 oz butter
3 pints stock
Salt, pepper, grated nutmeg
1 cup shelled peas
1 carrot
½ gill cream
2 oz flour

A fine photograph of Plymouth showing Derry's Clock and Theatre Royal Hotel in 1911. After bombing in the Second World War, the heart of Plymouth was rebuilt but the Barbican area retains much of its history, watched over by the Citadel, a fortress completed in the 1670s to guard Plymouth Sound.

Exmouth Devon Broth

METHOD

Peel onion and turnip, scrape carrot and wash the leek well by splitting open and running cold water through it. Shred the cabbage (separated leaf by leaf and well washed) and the leek. Chop finely the other vegetables including the parsley. Put the butter in a pan and quickly fry all the vegetables in it. Add the stock and simmer gently with the herbs and pearl barley, which should have soaked overnight. After adjusting seasoning, take out herbs and serve the soup very hot. Another lady referred to this basic vegetable soup as a Wintry Nights Soup. All these Devon soups are made superb by the quality of the stock and the freshness of the vegetables.

INGREDIENTS

1 quart mutton stock
1 onion
1 turnip
2 oz butter
A faggot of sweet herbs
Seasoning
1 cabbage heart
1 carrot
1 leek
3 oz pearl barley
A few sprigs of parsley

In October 1960, Paignton suffered severe flooding. This view of Paignton – Preston Beach and Sands – shows the calmer, sunny summer preceding the stormy, high winds.

Sidmouth Good Wife Soup

METHOD
Clean the leek well, removing outer leaves, and chop well. Peel and slice onion very thinly. Clean, peel and dice the potatoes. Melt butter in a pan and fry the cut-up vegetables in it gently for 5 minutes. Add the stock and nutmeg. Season and simmer for half an hour. Serve with toast sippets.

INGREDIENTS

1 quart good meat stock
2 oz butter
Pinch of nutmeg
Seasoning
2 medium sized potatoes
1 large leek
1 large Spanish onion

Sidmouth, one of the oldest resorts of South Devon, is considered the mildest. Much of the infancy of Queen Victoria was spent here. The Duke of Kent died here in 1820. Sidmouth is sheltered by hills 500 feet high. Its beautiful bay is flanked by High Peak in the west, and Salcombe Hill in the east. In this 1901 photograph can be seen the Bedford Hotel on the Esplanade. Agate, carnelian and jasper were to be found on the beach, where bathing was good. Rock pools and sea anemones delighted early visitors.

Exeter Spinach Soup

METHOD
Cook spinach in water for 8 minutes. Purée in a liquidiser or push through a hair sieve in the old-fashioned way. Reheat, slowly adding butter, pepper, salt and milk, stirring all the time to ensure a smooth consistency.

This is excellent before starting on the roast chicken.

INGREDIENTS

2 lb freshly picked, washed spinach
½ cup thin cream or top of milk
Freshly ground seasoning
½ teacup water
Knob of butter

Castle Drogo, of Drewsteignton near Exeter, was described as 'the last castle to be built in England'. Designed by Sir Edward Lutyens, it was the first twentieth-century property acquired by the National Trust. Major replanting of the garden, mingled with the wilderness of Dartmoor's granite scenery, means it is advisable to wear stout shoes and weatherproof clothing, but the spectacular views provided by the Teign Gorge make it all worthwhile. Plus homely soups from the National Trust kitchen. In 2007 the chapel roof was restored. Situated high in the Dartmoor National Park, Castle Drogo was built between 1911 and 1931 for Julius Drewe, a food retailing millionaire.

Castle Drogo, run by the National Trust, opened its doors to visitors early in 2008, with two special weekends in February. There will be a spring Trail and the Tea Room will have seasonal food such as delicious, warming home-made soup. There are breathtaking views far across Devon from the castle roof.

Hele's School at Southan near Exeter is well known. Hele Bay is in easy reach of Ilfracombe and in the village is an ancient restored watermill where visitors can buy wholemeal flour produced by this mill, which was originally built in 1525.

Sidbury Vegetable Marrow Soup

METHOD

Cut the vegetable marrow into cubes and place in stew pan with the chicken stock (preferably made by boiling chicken carcase), herbs, chopped celery heart, finely chopped onion. Boil gently for 2 minutes. Take out bunch of herbs and rub the soup through a sieve or liquidise. Return to stew pan, add milk and butter. Now adjust the seasoning with salt and black peppercorns, ground. Bring to the boil, sprinkle with the chives and serve with the diced toast fried crisply in the dripping. Old-fashioned sippets were made this way, beef or bacon dripping giving a good, meaty flavour. Cooked on low temperature, it takes ½ hour, serving six.

INGREDIENTS

2 lb vegetable marrow, without seeds and peel
1 celery heart
½ pint milk
1 teaspoon chopped chives
1 slice of toast
1 quart chicken stock
1 onion
Bunch of herbs
1 oz butter
2 oz dripping
Seasoning

The Old Bakery at Sidbury near Axminster was a draw not to be ignored amongst many other old and interesting buildings. Whitewashed cob, thatch and slate, Devonshire teas and honey at the Old Clock House added to its charms as did the Royal Oak with its high arch and mews, a relic of the old coaching days. Here we learned that the first Axminster carpet woven by a townsman, Thomas Whitty, was started on Midsummer Day, 1755.

Fish

Appledore Salmon Pie

METHOD

Bring the salmon to the boil in a pan containing water, wine, seasoning and bouquet garni. Make the pastry by rubbing 5 oz of butter into the two kinds of flour mixed together. Bind by adding just enough cold water to make a stiff dough. Roll out ⅔ of the pastry and with it line a loose-bottomed 9-inch cake tin. Mix together softened butter, anchovies, breadcrumbs, seasoning, blending all with the olive oil. Form this into balls. Fill the pie tin with salmon pieces and balls. With the remaining pastry make a lid for the pie. Make a hole in the centre. Bake in a moderate oven for 35 minutes. After 15 minutes pour ½ cup of the original cooking juices through the hole in the pastry lid. A good salad goes well with this salmon pie.

INGREDIENTS

½ lb fresh salmon tailpiece
1 sliced lemon
2 cups white wine
6 oz white flour
Salt, pepper and bouquet garni
6 oz wholemeal flour
2 oz butter
2 oz brown breadcrumbs
Olive oil
8 chopped anchovies

The quay at Appledore, around 1930.

There is evidence of salmon fishing in the River Torridge as far back as the ninth century. Walls built of sea cobbles and cobble gutters down the centre of streets, too narrow for cars and locally called 'drangs'. There are small courtyards. It is a charming village and was appreciated by no less than Elizabeth I, who made Appledore a free port for all shipping after the courage displayed by its sailors at the time of the Spanish Armada in 1588.

Appledore has been home to fishermen since Anglo-Saxon times and was yet another Devon town rewarded by Elizabeth I for sending ships and men to defeat the Spanish Armada.

The North Devon Maritime Museum reflects the town's seafaring history.

The once busy quay built alongside the River Torridge operates a passenger ferry to Instow during the holiday season. In July a regatta is held but bathing is not safe. Local craftsmen have built a replica of Drake's *Golden Hind*, the first ship to sail round the world.

Barnstaple Fish Stock

Fish soups were common in old Devon and the basis was a good fish stock, made as follows:

METHOD
Put all into a stew pan, bring to the boil and skim. Then simmer slowly for ¾ hour. Strain. Fish stock must be made freshly and used there and then.

The basis was also a 'hotch potch', shrimp and lobster shells could go in but no mackerel or salmon (too oily). All the trimmings were washed well and cut small, vegetables chopped small and herbs and spices put in a muslin bag.

INGREDIENTS

2 lb raw fish bones and trimming
6 white peppercorns
1 large onion
1 large tomato
½ teaspoon coarse salt
2 pints water
½ blade of mace
1 bay leaf and a sprig of parsley
1 small carrot

Sheltered moorings on the River Taw encouraged Barnstaple's development as a port. Merchants and ship owners met in Queen Anne's Walk, built in 1609, and like Bideford, Barnstaple has a bridge dating from the Middle Ages. The pannier market is famed for cream, butter and other local produce – also for its four-day fair in September.

Dartmouth Stewed Trout

METHOD

Clean the fish. Trim the scales off and remove fins and heads. Slit, rinse inside and pat dry. Melt the butter in a deep frying pan. Stir in flour, nutmeg and cayenne. Add the stock, lemon peel and parsley. Sprinkle the salt. Reduce the heat to a gentle simmer and cook, according to size of fish, from 15–30 minutes. Strain off the liquid, leaving a little to go with the fish and serve on warm dishes.

INGREDIENTS

2 medium-sized trout
3 oz butter
1 tablespoon flour
A pinch each of ground made, ground nutmeg and cayenne pepper
¼ pint chicken stock
A broad strip of lemon peel
Parsley sprigs
Salt

J. Smale took this photograph of Dartmouth over 100 years ago. Dartmouth is in the foreground with St Saviour's church standing out. On the other side of the river is Kingswear. A great sailing tradition lives on. In 1905, the *Britannia* training ship moored in the River Dart since 1863 was to be replaced with the Royal Naval College, associated with famous sea captains throughout history. Perhaps the most famous was dashing Sir Walter Raleigh.

Killerton Smoked Haddock with Poached Egg

METHOD

Cut haddock into small pieces and place in a buttered oven-proof dish with the onions, pepper and cream. Cook for a few minutes in a hot oven. Beat egg whites until they are very stiff. Pour over the haddock and cook just a few minutes in the oven until browned. Serve very hot.

INGREDIENTS

½ lb smoked haddock
½ cup cream
A pinch of cayenne pepper
½ teaspoon finely chopped onion
1 poached egg per person
Whites of 2 eggs

Torbay Mussels

Mussels were once found in large quantities. The shells should be tightly closed. If mussels float in water they are not fresh. The shells should be well washed and scrubbed, then soaked in salted water. Finally rinse under a running tap in a colander. Place the mussels wet into a strong, iron pan. Cover and place over a moderate fire. Keep shaking the pan. As soon as the mussels open they are ready. Strain off the liquor and keep for making fish stock. Turn the mussels out, beard them and serve on a white, damask napkin (the beard can be removed with scissors). Exmouth is the place for cockles.

Mussels made into a sauce for baked flounder and fresh grey sole or megrim and haddock were once popular in Devon, but the megrim has to be used as fresh as possible or it soon loses all flavour.

Beacon Cove, Torquay.

Baked Brown Trout

METHOD

Butter a fireproof dish, put in the washed trout, sprinkle with lemon juice and bake in a moderate oven for 20 minutes. The flavour of fresh river trout is so excellent that, like salmon, it needs no other flavouring or sauce.

Baked Teign Trout

METHOD

Clean trout and remove scales. Put the vinegar, thyme, chopped shallot and 3 tablespoons water into a pan with the seasoning and simmer for 5 minutes. Strain this liquid into an oven-proof baking dish and put in the trout. While cooking, baste well with the liquid over a period of ½ hour. Place the trout onto a hot dish. Sprinkle the teaspoon of flour into the liquor, add a nut of butter and stir until it boils. Keep stirring for 5 minutes more so that the flour cooks. Add the lemon juice. Pour over the fish and serve.

INGREDIENTS

4 small trout
1 shallot
1 teaspoon flour
Seasoning
1 tablespoon white
    vinegar
Sprig of thyme
1 teaspoon lemon juice

THE BOWLING GREEN, TEIGNMOUTH

'Trout tastes so wonderful because it feeds in the pure waters of the streams flowing from Exmoor' – this from a couple with 20 acres and fishing rights along a stretch of the River Mole.

View from the Salcombe Hotel.

Salmon Tail in Cream

METHOD
Butter an oven-proof dish. Put in the tail end and season
it well. Pour over the cider, sufficient to come half-way up
the sides of the dish and bake for ½ hour in a moderate
oven. Take out the fish, skin it and remove the bones. The
juices in which it was cooked should be rapidly boiled
to reduce quantity. Pour this over the fish and finish off
with the thick cream also poured. Another 10 minutes in
the oven and the salmon is ready to serve.

INGREDIENTS

1 tail end of salmon
¼ pint thick cream
Cider

Brixham Sole in Cider

METHOD
Place the fillets into an oven-proof dish. Pour the
cider over them and bake at 180° C for 30 minutes.
Strain the liquid into a saucepan and put in the
worked-together flour and butter. Cook for five
minutes until it thickens. Float in some snipped
chives and pour over the fillets of sole which have
meanwhile been kept warm. Torbay sole is noted for
quality and sometimes referred to as witch sole.

INGREDIENTS

4 fillets of sole
1 oz butter mixed with
1 teaspoon flour
½ pint cider
Seasoning
Chives

Old Brixham Harbour extended further inland so anchorage was protected on all sides. By the nineteenth century Brixham was the best-known fish market in the West of England. Narrow, cobbled alleys and long flights of stone steps featured in the old parts, one quaintness being 'ye olde Coffin House, only one in England'. In early 1900 it was used as a Shaving Saloon but in its long history it had changed from Coffee House to Coffin House!

Brixham Harbour. (Photograph by John T. Pullen)

Brixham sent fish to London and Bath in the eighteenth century and by the nineteenth was the best-known fish market in Devon. London-bound fish was sent by sea, but inland it was carried by pack horses.

Hancock's Devon Cider, one of four local ciders, is widely used. All are produced by traditional methods and have won over forty prizes.

Turbot in Cider

METHOD
Wash the turbot steaks and pat dry. Place in an oven-
proof dish spread with the mixed butter and chives,
then add cider, lemon juice and seasoning. Cover
and bake in a moderate oven for 25 minutes, basting
halfway through and at the end.

INGREDIENTS

4 turbot steaks
Squeeze of lemon
1 teaspoon chopped chives
½ pint Devon cider
2 oz butter
Seasoning

Bream with Egg Sauce

METHOD
Fresh fish is always stiff and firm, and any colours are
bright. A bream of 3 lb weight is suitable. Remove the
scales, scraping from tail to head with a knife. Cut off
the fins. Slit down the body and remove the inside.
The black skin on the inside of the fish should be
removed by rubbing with salt. Wash, and simmer
for 15 minutes in water containing 2 tablespoons of
tarragon vinegar.

   Melt the butter. Stir in the flour and milk and
stock and boil, stirring all the time. Cut the egg
in half, chopping the white. Add it to the sauce.
Season to taste. Boil for 3 minutes with the parsley
and pour the sauce over the fish, which should
meanwhile have been kept warm.

THE EGG SAUCE

1 hard-boiled egg
1½ oz flour
1 gill milk
1 dessertspoon chopped
   parsley
1½ oz butter
½ pint fish stock
Salt and pepper

Red Gurnard with Sauce

METHOD
Cook the flour in the melted butter, stirring well.
After 3 minutes add the fish stock, stirring all the
time. Remove from heat, stir in the strained egg
yolks and lemon juice. Season to taste and pour all
over the fish. The fish is skinned and boned and
poached gently in vinegar and water for 25 minutes,
after which it should be drained and flaked.

INGREDIENTS

1 red gurnard
1 tablespoon wholemeal
   flour
½ pint good fresh stock
2 egg yolks
1 tablespoon butter
Lemon juice
Seasoning

Bolt Head Marinated Herrings or Pilchards

METHOD

Clean and fillet the fish then roll them up and put into a porcelain dish. Add 3 bay leaves and 2 teaspoons of pickling spice, a little pepper and salt, then cover and bake slowly at 150° C for 2½ hours.

Some Devon housewives put a bay leaf into each rolled-up fish. The fish were left to go cold in the marinade.

INGREDIENTS

1 or 2 herrings
3 bay leaves
2 teaspoons pickling spice
Ground sea salt and black pepper

Bolt Head at Sunny Cove, Salcombe.

The coastguard station, Bolt Head, Salcombe. Crab fishing here draws the interest of some visitors. The National Trust is working on a project to support crab and lobster fishing on a sustainable level. The Trust casts a long shadow in South Cornwall and Devon, growing ever more popular. Menus in their restaurants may show vegetarian dishes (beetroot and leek tart), perhaps Beef Wellington, asparagus and salmon or fruit fools, made from local produce in season. No local, sun-ripened tomatoes? Then board green tomato chutney. Versatile!

Babbacombe Devonshire Pasty

METHOD

Make the pastry and let it rest in a cool pantry for an hour. Place the beaten eggs and milk in a basin. Make sure all bones are out of the fish and mix it in with the egg and milk. Add seasoning. Roll the pastry out and cut into rounds. Put filling into each round, pouring on a little of egg and milk mixed. Moisten edges of rounds and fit on a pastry top, crimping and sealing the pastry. Brush with more egg and bake in a moderate oven.

INGREDIENTS

6 oz cooked salmon
3 tablespoons milk
8 oz shortcrust pastry
2 beaten eggs
seasoning

Lover's Seat on Babbacombe Slopes. Maybe now, but it was once a haunt of smugglers. Excisemen raiding in 1853 found 153 casks of contraband spirits. The resort was popular before Torquay blossomed from a tiny fishing village. A steep hill descends from high cliffs to a sandy beach sheltered with a breakwater.

Shortcrust Pastry

METHOD

Sift the flour then rub in the lard lightly with the fingers until the mixture resembles breadcrumbs. Add the water carefully so that the resultant pastry is not sticky. It should come cleanly away from the bowl and feel soft.

INGREDIENTS

1 lb flour
6 tablespoons cold water
8 oz lard
A little milk

Kingswear Potted Buttered Crab meat

METHOD

The fresh white crab meat needs picking over carefully to remove any bits of shell. Place in a mixing bowl. Whip the brown crab meat into a paste. Add pepper and mix until smooth. Fold this into the white crabmeat. Melt the butter and when cool pour it onto the crab meat mixture, which can then be smoothed into ramekins. Put into the refrigerator until they are served, after pouring another thin layer of butter on each, to seal.

INGREDIENTS

About 1 lb crab meat (white)
9 oz crab meat (brown)
Pinch of salt
1 tablespoon virgin olive oil
About 5 oz butter
1 teaspoon cayenne pepper

We were told that a fleet of small boats off Kingswear land crabs worth £1 million a year so a recipe had to be found!

'Crabbers', an 1870 engraving of Devon fishermen catching crabs.

We enjoyed a trip on the Dart Valley Railway Company's steam-hauled Torbay and Dartmouth Line, which was originally part of the Great Western Railway in 1864.

Devonshire pasties can also be filled with fruit, apple pasty seemingly being the most popular, but 1989 was a wonderful summer for apples. Markets at South Molton, Tiverton, Newton Abbot, Bideford, Barnstaple etc. were loaded with Cox's, Lord Lambourne, Russet, Bramley, Charles Ross.

Laver Pickle

METHOD
Laver used to be and maybe still is grown at Barnstaple, where we found it selling briskly in Eric Hayes' shop. He advised that it be used freshly and explained, 'Gather the flat, green, filmy, ribbon-like laver [seaweed] preferably from rocks. Wash it well. Place it in a saucepan with vinegar and butter. Boil it, until it thickens. Put in jars. At one time the pickle was sealed with mutton fat. Eat with Hogs Pudding.' Laver collected from sand is difficult to clean.

In 'the farthest corner of Devon' lies Welcombe, 18 miles from Bideford. To the south flows a stream where Cornwall begins. Cottages and farms are built of stone and cob. Earth and stone hedges abound. They seem to grow out of the landscape. Here we discovered Devon beef stew – six vegetables, spices and bay leaf plus meat, all in one pot.

Barnstaple from the South Walk, a 1902 photograph by Vickery brothers taken at the head of the estuary of River Taw, which is spanned by a bridge of sixteen arches dating from the thirteenth century. The ruins of an ancient castle are marked with a 'keep mound'. Barnstaple was the centre of trade for North Devon.

Trawler-man's son Peter Taylor, who caught all kinds of fish (except halibut) in the Bay, told us he had caught eels up to 100 lb in weight and that another Barnstaple meal was …

Saltwater Eels

METHOD
Discard tail and bottom half. Cleanse, cut in pieces and simmer. Skin, then bake in a dish with bay leaves and spices, using 50 per cent water, 50 per cent vinegar.

Baked Turbot

METHOD

Wash the fish, rub with a little sea salt, dry, and dust the fish with seasoned flour. Coat with beaten egg and breadcrumbs and put the fish in a buttered baking dish, cutting the leftover butter into little pieces and scattering on the fish. Serve with the hot shrimp sauce, which is basically made by shelling and pounding up the shrimps and then adding gradually to a cornflour sauce.

For advice on cooking, especially with old recipes, Mrs Beeton still reigns supreme and she praised turbot as 'a very nourishing fish of excellent flavour with firm, creamy white flesh'. Choose the middle cut as there is no waste. 'The fins of turbot should never be cut off. They were once considered a great delicacy.'

INGREDIENTS

2 thin slices from a thick turbot
Baked breadcrumbs
1 tablespoon flour
1 egg
½ pint shrimp sauce
1 oz butter
Salt and pepper

Salcombe, with one of the finest harbours in the West Country, is still a favourite with yachtsmen. Its first regatta was held in 1857. On 4 June 1944 thousands of Americans set off from Salcombe to participate in the D-Day Landings, a historic event commemorated by a plaque in Normandy Way.

The old custom of gathering winkles on a Good Friday was considered lucky in Devon. The area of Torbay was famed for its fish. Around Easter, limpet pies were made, rather like mince pies with sugar, spice and dried fruits but containing a limpet in the centre. Life revolved around the sea, a dangerous calling made apparent in Brixham by the monument erected in the churchyard in memory of 100 sailors who perished in a storm in 1866, when forty ships were driven onto rocks.

Tiverton Salmagundi

This recipe probably found its way from Lancashire when cheese was sent south on the schooners from small, now forgotten ports, returning with Somerset or Devon slate as ballast. Recipes do cross county boundaries. This from the Moorcock Inn in the bleak Pennines surfaced in Tiverton.

INGREDIENTS

8 oz sliced, smoked salmon
Chopped parsley
2 oz melted butter
Lemon juice
Ground black pepper
Sea salt to taste

METHOD
Lay 4 oz of the salmon flat on a greased greaseproof paper to form a rectangle. Put the rest of the salmon into a blender with all the other ingredients until a smooth paste is formed. Season and place this mixture into the centre of your rectangle. Roll tightly and refrigerate for 2 hours until it is firm. Slice with a hot knife and serve garnished with cucumber or watercress.

'Salomangundy', said to go back to the sixteenth century and attributed to a lady-in-waiting at the court of Henry IV of France, was the mixture of minced veal, chicken or turkey, with anchovies or pickled herrings and onions, chopped fine, served with lemon juice and olive oil. By the eighteenth century anchovies were considered an essential ingredient.

Rocks Off Devon painting by Peter Graham RA, 1885. Like the natural arch 'London Bridge' not far from Meadfoot Beach, it was made by the waves' surge over hundreds of years. The two black birds (right) are shags, they are together on the lower rock. Fulmar and Kittiwakes are among the rest of the birds. 'Ribbed and paled in with rocks unscalable and roaring waters.' This well describes this part of Devon.

Meat and Savoury Dishes

Roman Pie

This is a wartime recipe from actor John Gielgud in 1942, the year of the blockade. From a book printed during the Second World War by the Devon Athaeneum.

METHOD
Break the spaghetti into pieces about 2 inches long. Boil in salted water for about 20 minutes; let it go cold. Cut the meat or game into fine pieces (do not mince it), line a cake tin with very thin pastry and fill it with alternate layers of meat, spaghetti, cheese and seasoning, spaghetti and cheese on top. Moisten well with stock and cream (white sauce). Cover with a thin layer of pastry dough. Sprinkle with a little vermicelli and a light sprinkle of cheese and bake for about 30 minutes in a hot oven. The cheese thickens the stock as it cooks, and it is well to have a little sauce to hand in case the mixture is not quite moist enough. It can be made in a fire-proof glass dish with only a pastry crust if preferred.

INGREDIENTS

8 oz cooked meat, veal or pork, rabbit, fowl or pheasant
4 oz spaghetti
¼ pint stock and a little cream or white sauce
2 oz grated cheese
some thinly rolled pastry

Appledore Parsnip Cakes

This recipe came from a country pub, which served the cakes with Sunday roast.

METHOD
Peel and clean the parsnips, boiling in water until soft. Drain and mash them thoroughly. Add the flour, seasoning and butter. Mix well and form into flat, round cakes. Dip in beaten egg and scatter with the breadcrumbs. Fry on both sides until nicely browned. They are made in much the same way as Lancashire potato cakes.

INGREDIENTS

1 lb parsnips
2 tablespoons flour
1 breakfast cup breadcrumbs
1 beaten egg
Seasoning
1 oz butter

Dartmouth and Okehampton Devon Sausage

METHOD

Chop the pork finely or mince it coarsely with the fat and bacon. Mix in the breadcrumbs and season well with the salt, pepper, spices and herbs. Grease a baking sheet with a little lard. Shape or pipe the mixture into a long, continuous roll about 2 cm thick and coil up on the sheet. Melt the lard and brush the sausage very lightly with it. Bake in a warm oven, 160° C for 30–45 minutes or until the sausage is cooked through. Drain off the fat and serve cut in short lengths. (Courtesy Andrea of Ashfarm Dairy)

INGREDIENTS

1 lb lean shoulder of pork
150 g pork fat
1 rasher of smoked bacon, without rind
50 g wholemeal breadcrumbs
1 x 5 ml spoon salt
1 x 2.5 ml spoon pepper
Large pinch of ground mace
Large pinch of grated nutmeg
Half a 2.5 ml spoon dried thyme (optional)
Quarter of a 2.5 ml spoon dried, crushed safe (optional)
Lard

Six girls from Arnold High School, Blackpool, on a Sea Cadets course at Dartmouth, September 1966.

On the River Dart, naval vessels, pleasure yachts, trawlers and ferries are to be seen, the latter crossing between Dartmouth and Kingswear. There have been many historic sailings from here: the crusades in 1147 and an American fleet in 1944, which left on D-Day. This photograph of Dartmouth's unspoiled river front was taken in 1924.

THE RIVER AT DARTMOUTH CASTLE.

Okehampton March Fair displayed almost every commodity to the crowds: livestock; gingerbreads; fruit and vegetables; meat; fish; clothing; even patent medicines. Bampton Fair, held every October, when Exmoor ponies are rounded up, is perhaps the most famous horse fair in the land. Devon markets always drew large crowds.

The magnificent door on the church of St Saviour, Dartmouth, is clearly dated 1631 but the iron figures of the beasts guarding the symbolic Tree of Life are thought to be even earlier. In many such ancient churches provision for a 'dole' of bread was often made in the wills of rich parishioners, the loaves to be given to the poor, needy and old who came to church.

Paignton Stewed Ox Kidney

METHOD

Skin and core the kidney and cut it into thin rounds. Heat 2 tablespoons of butter in a frying pan and brown the kidney slices on both sides quickly. Do not overcook. Add mushrooms, parsley and onions, tossing them in the butter. Put in the rest of the butter, seasoning well. Sprinkle in the flour and stir in the sauce and lemon juice. Very slowly, pour on the stock and stir over low heat for 6 minutes. Serve hot with the sippets, and a vegetable if desired.

INGREDIENTS

1–1¼ ox kidney
3 tablespoons butter
2 oz mushrooms, well chopped
2 tablespoons parsley
1 small onion, chopped
Salt and pepper
1 tablespoon flour
2 teaspoons Lazenby's Anchovy Essence (sauce can be substituted)
1 teaspoon lemon juice
¼ pint beef stock of water
Sippets

A late-eighteenth-century bottled essence, Lazenby's Anchovy Essence was created by an innkeeper, Peter Harvey, and his sister, Elizabeth Lazenby. It was popular in this recipe and many others and was joined in the Victorian era by Harvey's sauce. Later on came canned fruits and vegetables, packaged foods such as Bird's Custard and Kellogg's Toasted Corn Flakes, 'the sweetheart of the corn', all being very helpful to the busy housewife.

This 1900s postcard of Paignton was from at a time when many improvements were afoot. A very old town, belonging to the See of Exeter before the Norman Conquest, it was also famous as a place where cider was manufactured on a large scale. In springtime visitors came for miles to see the apple blossom.

Parsnips in Dripping

METHOD

Wash and peel parsnips and cut into thick slices. Boil for 10 minutes then strain off the water. Heat the beef or pork dripping in a pan and gently slide in the parsnips. Cook until tender and brown. This takes another 10 minutes. Sprinkle with seasoning and serve with slices of boiled beef.

INGREDIENTS

4 parsnips
2 oz dripping
seasoning

The 'dogs of Devon', under Sir Francis Drake, routed the Spanish Armada, but tempestuous seas driven by high winds helped towards that total defeat. From the wrecked galleons, massive timbers were used to put into buildings that can still be seen today. Armada Bullion chests were washed up. One example is at Saxey's Hospital, Bruton. The hospital and a school dating from 1889 were generously endowed by a boy of Bruton, once a poor boy.

Sir Francis Drake, besides being a brilliant seaman, was Mayor of Plymouth and the first Englishman to sail round the world. A model of his famous ship the *Golden Hind* is preserved at Brixham.

How to Tenderise Cheaper Cuts of Beef

METHOD

Wipe meat and cut into 5 pieces. Chop onions. Heat up dripping and quickly brown the pieces of meat in it (2 minutes). After removing the meat to a hot plate, fry the onions, adding more beef dripping if necessary. Put the meat in a double saucepan covered with cold water and cook slowly. After 20 minutes add the washed rice, onions and bunch of herbs. Simmer all for 2½ hours and serve with the tomatoes as vegetable, slicing and cooking these also in beef dripping and arranging them round the meat with boiled potatoes and watercress garnish.

INGREDIENTS

1 lb buttock steak
1 lb tomatoes
Bunch of herbs
1 oz dripping
Salt and pepper
2 onions
1 oz rice
½ pint cold water
1 tablespoon meat stock

Roast Partridge in Sherry Sauce

METHOD

Divide the coked partridges into joints. Heat butter in a large pan, add mushrooms, carrot, onion, bay leaf, parsley, thyme and ham. Gently fry then sprinkle with flour. Stir in stock and sherry and simmer until liquid is reduced by ⅓. Add the partridge pieces, gently cook on for about 10 minutes. Serve hot with a watercress and tomato side salad.

INGREDIENTS

2 roasted partridges
2 oz mushrooms
1 bay leaf
½ teaspoon thyme
1 oz flour
1 pint chicken stock
2 oz butter
1 small onion, finely chopped
1 small carrot, finely chopped
1 level tablespoon chopped parsley
4 oz lean chopped ham
⅓ pint sherry

Meadfoot Beach and Beacon Cove. 'This is our favourite cove,' Lil wrote to Mrs Winfield on 7 August 1931. She meant Beacon Cove but both Meadfoot and Beacon were popular. Strawberries, pots of tea and thickly buttered Devonshire scones were available at both. (Photograph by Sweetman & Son).

Ilfracombe Celery Stuffing

METHOD

Use the heart of the celery as the outer stalk will be stringy. Mix all ingredients together and bind with the beaten egg.

INGREDIENTS

1 teacup chopped celery
¼ lb breadcrumbs
3 oz shredded suet
1 tablespoon chopped parsley
1 teaspoon finely chopped nuts
Grated lemon rind
1 egg

The *Around Britain Guide* in 1902 advised, 'Having a good natural harbour, long since furnished with two piers and a good quay, Ilfracombe is a port of some antiquity; but of late years its growth as a fashionable watering-place has been phenomenal. It possesses the charms of bold cliffs, clear sea and grand scenery around, and the balmy yet bracing climate of North Devon. Our view shows clearly the general plan of the town. In the middle of the picture is the bold bluff of the Capstone Hill, with the walks cut round it, and at its foot is a spacious pavilion, and near the foreground is Lantern Hill, overlooking the harbour. Terraces and walks are cut along or under the cliffs on both sides of the town.' The hills seen are known as the Tors.

The famous paddle steamer *Waverley* made trips from Ilfracombe in summer. This view from 1927 shows Hillsborough Hill, Ilfracombe.

Chestnut Stuffing

METHOD

This is easily made once you have got your chestnuts. The shells and skins can be removed by scalding or placing in a hot oven until the skins split. Boil them until tender. Mash them or put through a sieve. Mix them with melted butter, chopped parsley, breadcrumbs and seasoning, then bind with a well-beaten egg, much as is done with celery and onion stuffing. Chestnut stuffing is good with the Christmas turkey.

Ilfracombe Redcurrant Sauce for Roast Lamb

METHOD

Pour off the liquid from the baking tin, being careful to retain all the brown sediment which is so tasty. Add half a pint of hot water and stir well. Add butter, salt and pepper, then stir in the redcurrant jelly and the strained lemon juice and simmer the sauce for 5 minutes.

INGREDIENTS

½ lemon
½ pint gravy from roasted lamb
2 ½ tablespoons redcurrant jelly
1 oz butter
Salt and pepper

A happy holiday scene when George V was on the throne. Lantern Hill, Ilfracombe was photographed in July 1928. 'My dear Brighteye,' reads this card, ' ... glorious weather and there is plenty of good tucker.' North Devon's largest holiday resort developed in the nineteenth century, but it had been a safe haven for fishing boats for a long time, Ilfracombe's sheltered harbour being at the foot of craggy Lantern Hill.

Paignton Scalloped Mushrooms

METHOD

Grease scallop shells with butter. Melt butter in pan and add chopped mushrooms, diced ham and onion. Cook gently for 5 minutes. Take this mixture out of pan, leaving in the butter, if necessary add a little more butter. Put in the flour, stir well and cook. Remove from heat and add chicken stock, stirring well into the cooked flour, then add milk, seasoning and lemon juice. Return to heat until it thickens, then add to the mushroom mixture, stirring well. Place portions in scallop shells. Sprinkle with dried breadcrumbs and brown under grill. Garnish with parsley or watercress.

INGREDIENTS

8 oz mushrooms
1 tablespoon chopped onion
2 oz flour
¼ pint chicken stock
4 oz diced ham
2 oz butter
¼ pint milk
4 tablespoons dried
    breadcrumbs

Pier End and Promenade, Paignton.

Cheese and Bacon Scones

METHOD

Rub fat into flour and baking powder. Add 3 oz finely grated cheese, 3 rashers of cooked, finely chopped bacon. Bind with 6 tablespoons milk. Roll out 1 inch in thickness. Cut into scones and brush the tops with egg. Bake in a hot oven about 12 minutes. Serve hot, slit and spread with savoury butter.

INGREDIENTS

8 oz self-raising flour
¼ teaspoon dry mustard
Sprinkle of pepper
1 heaped teaspoon baking powder
¼ teaspoon salt
2 oz margarine
3 rashers of cooked, finely chopped bacon

SAVOURY BUTTER

Using either 1 large, skinned, chopped tomato or 2 oz grated cheese, beat in 2 oz soft, seasoned butter.

Cadhay is not mentioned in the Domesday Book but it appears first in the reign of Edward I as part of the manor of Ottery St Mary. The Haydon family who took over Cadhay was headed by a successful lawyer, John Cadhay Haydon.

John and his wife Joan were living there before 1545 and they built the bridge between Cadhay and Ottery and it bore a typical Tudor inscription:

John and Joan built me,
Pray good people repair me.

Sadly they had no children, and in 1587 Cadhay passed to Robert Haydon. The most striking architectural feature of Cadhay is the Court of Sovereigns. The wall treatment in the Courtyard is patterned with sandstone and flint, a style then in use in East Anglia. Over the doors of the Courtyard are statues of Henry VIII, Edward VI, Mary and Elizabeth I.

Risdon, in his survey of Devon in 1620, wrote, 'John Haydon of Cadhay builded a fair new house.'

The saddle tank engine *Magpie*, which was built in 1861, is standing here at St Ives. We had a lovely ride on the branch line in 1950, it being the last section of railway designed for running on the broad gauge track used by engineer Isambard Kingdom Brunel. A must for railway enthusiasts!

Statue of Henry VIII at Cadhay. The surrounding walls show the 'Sovereign Courtyard' treatment of alternating flint and sandstone.

Bowden's Guide Book, the year the outer harbour at Torquay was photographed, declared that 'it was a very desirable place as well as a place to spend a holiday', 'Leisure Land' was what the *Standard* newspaper said. The new sea wall enclosed 30 acres, giving safe anchorage for yachts and it caused more sand to accumulate on Torre Abbey Beach, which the children approved of! Union Street housed large mercantile premises. The Prince of Wales, later Edward VII, attended Torquay's famous annual regatta.

Tiverton Meat Loaf

METHOD

Mix all together. Line a 1 lb loaf tin with foil. Pack
in the mixture with a buttered paper on top, which
should be removed after 1¼ hours at 180° C. Then
cook on for a further ¼ hour.

Sliced up cold, this made a good snack for workmen
but served hot, it can be accompanied with chopped
spring cabbage or mashed carrots and turnips.

INGREDIENTS

¾ lb lean minced beef
½ cup porridge oats
4 oz grated carrot
½ Spanish onion, grated
1 teaspoon sauce or
    chutney
Salt and pepper
1 egg to bind

Left: A table of tolls payable at a turnpike gate. Any
coach drawn by more than one horse paid four pence
and a halfpenny.

Below: St Mary's Abbey, Buckfast. The French Benedictine
monks that acquired the site in 1882 worked in groups
of four to six. It took thirty-one years to finish the main
building. Visitors can visit tea rooms and a museum of
shells and are enthralled by the singing of Gregorian chants.
Stately homes such as Chudleigh, Bradley Manor, Mearsden
Manor and Powderham Castle are within reach.

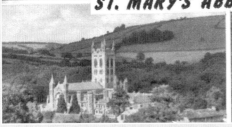

ST. MARY'S ABBEY, BUCKFAST

R. D. Blackmore's famous novel *Lorna Doone* grew from his early experiences of North Devon and Somerset, strengthened by the famous Blundell's School at Tiverton (nearby Dulverton was the home of uncle Reuben Huckaback in the story). The opening scene in *Lorna Doone* is based on Blundell's, where a fight is going on between the young John Ridd and another schoolboy. So famous has the novel become, the area is known as *Lorna Doone* country.

Part of *Lorna Doone* was written at the Royal Oak Inn at Winsford and the story was first published in 1869.

Old Blundell's School, Tiverton.

The famous clapper bridge at Tarr Steps crosses the River Barle west of Dulverton. Although very old it is no longer thought to be prehistoric, but a lovely part of Exmoor.

Greenway Ham and Mushroom Omelette

METHOD

Wash and peel mushrooms and cook them on low gas in butter. Gently shake the pan. Time not more than 7 minutes. Add the jar of shrimps and the ham cut into small pieces. Keep warm. Break the eggs into a bowl and beat with a fork. Add the seasoning. Pour this into a large heated frying pan and stir for a few minutes. The eggs soon set. Do not overcook. Quickly place the warm filling on one side of the omelette. Fold over the other side. Serve at once.

INGREDIENTS

½ lb mushrooms
Jar of shrimps
5 eggs
Salt and pepper
1 dessertspoon olive oil
¼ lb cooked ham
Butter

Greenway House in wooded grounds was the birthplace of Sir Humphrey Gilbert, the seafarer who claimed Newfoundland for Queen Elizabeth I. The house became the home of Agatha Christie from 1938 until her death in 1976.

The Pilchard Inn on Burgh Island, Bigbury-on-Sea – 'Agatha Christie country'. The quay at Greenway was bought by the National Trust in 2005 as 'green access for the garden'. This area was loved by Agatha Christie, the famous detective story writer, for its atmosphere of timeless tranquillity. I was told that this recipe was a favourite of hers. It is quite delicious.

Plymouth Lamb and Chestnuts

METHOD

The lamb should be boned and the meat cut into pieces. Skin the chestnuts. Melt the butter in a heavy pan. Brown the lamb in this. Lower heat and put in the stock. Bring slowly to the boil. Add the thyme and marjoram and replace the lamb. Cover the pan and leave on low heat for 35 minutes.

INGREDIENTS

1 shoulder of lamb
1 oz butter
1 tablespoon chopped lemon and thyme
½ pint stock
8 oz chestnuts
1 large sliced onion
1 tablespoon chopped marjoram

Green Lantern Restaurant, New Street, Plymouth, August 1970. Mayflower 70 commemorated the 350th anniversary of the sailing of the Pilgrim Fathers from Plymouth, England, to Plymouth, New England.

As fierce, marauding brigands haunted and held terrifying sway over the lonely parts of Exmoor, the Gubbins gang of Dartmoor were feared, well over a century before the Doones. Their habit was to intercept sailors crossing the moor from Plymouth to Bideford in Elizabethan times. Another author, Charles Kingsley, tells of them in his book, *Westward Ho!*

In an area of Dartmoor like this is to be found the Nun's Cross, giving some idea of the vastness and wild quality of the Moor. Covering an area of 365 square miles, it is the southernmost National Park in Great Britain. Left from the Neolithic Period onwards, tombs, hut circles, standing crosses and stones are found on Dartmoor, indicating past civilisations. 'Devon for Sun' was the 1950s slogan.

Plymouth Potato and Cheese Cakes

METHOD

Mix all the ingredients well together. On a greased griddle or the base of a thick frying pan press small, rounded quantities of this mixture. Cook over gentle heat, turning to brown on the other side or these potato and cheese cakes can be baked on a greased baking sheet in the oven at 200° C for 15 minutes.

INGREDIENTS

10 oz cooked mashed potato
1 level teaspoon dry mustard
4 oz finely grated cheese
1 teaspoon ground sea salt
1 egg, well beaten

In the days of the Pilgrim Fathers, men known as Oggie Eaters collected for charity in Plymouth with a large box supported by poles. The collecting box was shaped like an 'Oggie', a pasty filled with onion, chopped meat and turnip, similar to the Cornish pasties so popular in Cornwall.

Ladram Bay Chestnut Savoury

METHOD

Slit the chestnuts on the flat side and put them in a tin in a hot oven for 15 minutes. When the shells begin to split open, remove and peel off inner skins. Boil the chestnuts for 20 minutes and strain off water. Mash them and place in a pan with 1½ oz butter, mustard and herbs. Add the flour and mix well. Put in the milk and stir until it boils. Season and add nearly all the cheese and a well-beaten egg. Put into a fireproof dish and sprinkle with the rest of the cheese. Dot bits of butter on top and bake for 10 minutes in a hot oven. This is very good with watercress and sliced tomatoes.

INGREDIENTS

1 lb chestnuts
1 egg
¼ teaspoon mixed dried herbs
2 oz grated cheese
seasoning
2 oz butter
1 oz flour
¼ teaspoon mustard
1 gill milk

Ladram Bay, one of Devon's secluded beaches and a fine example of red sandstone cliffs. There are caves to explore and isolated stacks are frequented by many sea birds.

Exeter Stew

METHOD
The sliced onions are cooked in the beef dripping, then put the stock and cider in with the cubed, floured meat. Let it simmer for a while then put in the marjoram and chopped vegetables. Season well and simmer gently for 2 hours, by which time the meat should be tender.

This stew was accompanied by dumplings, which were put into the pot ½ hour before the stew was ready, enough time to cook them and imbue with a beefy flavour.

These were made as follows:

METHOD
Mix the dry ingredients and bind with a little water. Do not make the dough sticky. Roll into 6 small balls and drop them into the Exeter Stew. At North Morton these were referred to as 'pretty dumplings'.

INGREDIENTS

2 lb cubed shoulder steak, rolled in seasoned flour
2 large Spanish onions, sliced thinly
1 pint good beef stock
3 stalks washed celery or chopped celery heart
½ teaspoons marjoram
Some beef dripping
½ lb parsnip, cut up
½ pint Devon cider
Seasoning

THE DUMPLINGS

4 oz flour
A good pinch of mixed herbs
Water
2 oz shredded suet
Seasoning

In the Cathedral Close in Exeter is Moll's Coffee House, built 1596 and having an Elizabethan oak-panelled room. A frieze shows the armorial bearings of famous Elizabethans; Drake, Raleigh and Gilbert. Over the door, a carving declares, 'The meeting place of our naval and military generals who fought with the Spanish Armada.' Edgar Ward's photo from the 1920s reveals that a picture framer and gilder Worth & Company occupy the ground-floor premises.

To Prepare Rice for Curry

METHOD

Half fill a clean pan with boiling water seasoned with salt. Place in the quantity of rice required. Boil quickly for 15 minutes, stirring with a clean, wooden spoon. Strain through a colander and run cold water on the rice to separate the grains. Let it drip, then after a few minutes put colander in empty stewpan and stand near the fire, turning lightly to make it free and dry. It can be served round curry or as a separate dish with meat instead of potatoes.

The meat served with rice was often in the form of mutton chops, stewed with a large onion and seasoning. Mutton was considered more wholesome than beef, especially for patients recovering from illness. If roasted, it was set before the fire and basted constantly. What was known as Roast Gigot of Mutton was cooked in an iron stewpan and needed less attention.'Two hours should cook a seven-pound leg of mutton.'

This recipe from Devonport came from my Devon sister-in-law, Josephine Houghton.

Cremyll near Devonport.

Exmouth Toad in the Hole

METHOD
Place butter and sausages in a 10-inch by 12-inch roasting tin and cook on 220° C for 10 minutes. Sift the flour and break the egg into it. Gradually add half the milk, beating well, then add the rest to keep the mixture smooth. Pour the batter into the roasting tin and bake for 45 minutes. The batter will then be risen and golden in colour. Before adding the batter, carefully pour off excess sausage fat.

INGREDIENTS

1 oz butter
1 lb sausages
4 oz flour
1 egg
¼ pint fresh milk

Maiden Combe Beach.

Dawlish Warren Jugged Hare with Redcurrant Jelly

METHOD

Melt the butter and mix all in to form the marinade; the onion should be very thinly sliced. The washed, jointed hare must be placed in the marinade and turned several times during the 2 days. Having removed the hare joints from the marinade, pat dry and gently brown in butter. Place them in a deep, oven-proof dish with a layer of finely chopped vegetables at the bottom (celery, carrot, onion, parsley) just enough to cover the dish. Scatter more chopped parsley and fresh thyme mixed with 1 tablespoon of flour over the joints. Add water until it comes ¾ way up the pot. Cover tightly and cook in a moderate oven for 3 hours. Half an hour before cooking time is up, stir in 3 tablespoons of redcurrant jelly.

THE MARINADE

1 glass tarragon vinegar
1 onion, sliced
3 bay leaves
2 oz butter
1 glass Devon cider
4 crushed juniper berries
Salt and pepper

This is traditionally served on Boxing Day, the hare left marinating in the cold pantry for two days prior to cooking. Some like to thicken the hare gravy with cornflour, but my father, who took his cooking seriously, never did this. He served jugged hare with freshly pickled, hot red cabbage. He was, however, a Lancashire man and not a Devonshire man.

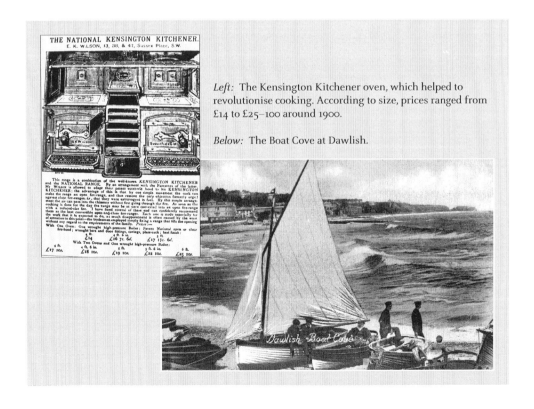

Left: The Kensington Kitchener oven, which helped to revolutionise cooking. According to size, prices ranged from £14 to £25–100 around 1900.

Below: The Boat Cove at Dawlish.

Princetown Hog's Pudding

METHOD

Mix all ingredients together, making sure that the
herbs are evenly distributed. With floured hands
shape the meat into sausages. Dust with more flour.
Put to stand in a cold place and cook after 3 hours,
either frying or, if the mixture is to be baked, in
small, greased tins. Do not overfill the tins. Place
in a moderate oven for about 20 minutes. The
pudding can also go into pasties with the addition
of chopped onion and turnip.

INGREDIENTS

2 lb belly of pork, minced
1 teaspoon dried sage
salt and black pepper
8 oz fresh breadcrumbs
½ teaspoon thyme

This recipe could have been used for the convicts' meals. There were old
postcards showing the prisoners being drilled and stone-breaking in Princetown.

Some of the best recipes for this traditional Devon dish have been handed down
over the generations by pork butchers and are well-guarded secrets. Here is one
of them. Soak some sausage pig skins in salted water. Mix together minced pork,
breadcrumbs and a sprinkling of mixed herbs. Season thoroughly with salt and
pepper. Fill the skins with this mixture and tie the ends of each tightly. Boil until
cooked. Hog's pudding is delicious, sliced and eaten cold, fried with bacon, bread or
egg, or even put into a pasty.

The prison at Princetown was originally built in 1806 for French prisoners of war, but became a criminal
prison in 1850. From Dartmoor, granite was sent to build the famous Nelson's Column and London
Bridge. A horse-drawn tramway took stone down to Teignmouth, where it was shipped southwards.

Roast Duck and Chestnuts – A Favourite at Devon Hotels

METHOD

The stuffing is made by cutting a slit in each chestnut and boiling in water for 15 minutes. Drain and peel. Melt the butter and sweat the chopped celery heart in it. Add the chestnuts, about ½ pint of the hot water, season and simmer on for 15 minutes, keeping the mixture well stirred.

    The prepared duck should be wiped inside after washing, and stuffed with the chestnut and celery mixture. Prick the skin of the duck all over and place in a roasting tin. Roast at 200°C for 2 hours, with greaseproof paper protecting the duck. Baste and remove the greaseproof towards end of cooking allowing about ½ hour for it to brown. The remaining hot water can top up the juices in the tin. Bring to table garnished with the parsley.

    Going back three centuries, food prices were very different. A leg of mutton cost two pence, geese were six pence each and nineteen chickens could be had for one shilling and eight pence.

INGREDIENTS

1 lb chestnuts
1 pint hot water
1 duck about 6 lb weight
Sprigs of washed parsley to garnish
2 oz butter
Seasoning
1 chopped onion
1 celery heart

Okehampton Roast Beef and Gherkins and Suet Pudding

More than 1,300 years ago the farmers used to fatten their cattle in such rich pastures, these were known in Saxon times as the summer Land.

    The Baron of beef was equivalent to the 'saddle' in lamb and consisted of a double sirloin. To make it tender the beef was well hung then put in a large baking tin in a hot oven. After 15 minutes the heat was reduced and the meat basted regularly every quarter of an hour. This was considered very important. One quarter of an hour cooking time was allowed for each pound, plus an additional quarter. In older kitchens a meat jack would be used to suspend the meat for the roasting. The rich sediment of gravy was always served with the beef. The fat was poured into a pan in which slices of plain suet roll were browned, ready to serve round the meat.

METHOD

Put the yolk of an egg in a basin with a quarter of a teaspoon of mustard mixed with a little cream. Add, drop by drop, enough salad oil to form a thick paste. Stir in a tablespoon of finely chopped gherkins.

THE SAUCE

1 egg yolk
¼ teaspoon mustard
Cream
Salad Oil
1 tablespoon finely chopped gherkins

Purists visit Throwleigh for its 'long straw thatching', an ancient craft seen at its best in Devon. It contrasts so beautifully with Dartmoor granite. Six miles from Gidleigh, which has a Mariners Way, we were told this path was used by sailors as the shorter route to Bideford where, belated and worse for drink, they joined their ships.

Tavistock Pheasant with Apple Sauce

METHOD

My grandmother wrapped the breast of the prepared bird with rashers of streaky bacon and placed it with the butter in the roasting tin. Determine the weight, allowing 20 minutes to the lb and 15 minutes over, cooking in a moderate oven. The bird was covered with folded, dampened graseproof paper as well, which was lifted for basting purposes during cooking, then replaced, but removed entirely 15 minutes before the end.

METHOD

Melt the butter and place in the peeled, cored, sliced apples. Stew very gently indeed. The apples should not fall, the secret being to slice them very thinly; thus they will keep their shape. Add a pinch of cinnamon and finally the cider. Simmer on over low heat until the sauce thickens. Serve hot with the roast pheasant.

INGREDIENTS

1 large pheasant (hung for 3 days)
2 tablespoons butter

THE APPLE SAUCE

1 lb apples
1 oz butter
¼ pint cider
Pinch of cinnamon

Tavistock, about 10 miles from Plymouth, became a mining centre in the eighteenth century when copper was discovered and transported along a canal to the Tamar river. With so much copper and bronze, Tavistock has a statue of Sir Francis Drake, who was born in the vicinity.

Stoke Gabriel Lamb Stew

METHOD
Place the lamb, garlic and sherry in a large mixing
bowl. Combine well and leave to marinate for 4
hours. Remove the lamb, pat dry and save the
marinade. Sprinkle the lamb with salt, pepper and
cumin. Place the oil in a large saucepan. Add the
pieces of lamb and fry them for 5 minutes with the
onions. Pour over the marinade and bring to the
boil. Reduce to a simmer and with the pan covered,
simmer the stew for 1½ hours. Serve very hot with
crusty bread rolls and watercress.

INGREDIENTS

3 lb boned lamb, cubed
2 crushed garlic cloves
1 teaspoon ground cumin
4 tablespoons vegetable
  oil
2 medium onions, sliced
½ teaspoon salt
½ teaspoon black pepper
1½ cups dry sherry

An ancient quality lingers in Stoke Gabriel, yet it seems 'up to the minute'! All
admire the 'shute' – Combe Shute, a lane snaking through the village with its
white cottages, sea shell patterns, and a grand profusion of flowers. Church House
Inn welcomes, and it is only 5 miles from Totnes.

Exmouth Summer Herb Tart

METHOD
Sieve the flour and rub in the butter, using a deep
baking bowl. Mix to a dough with the egg yolk
and milk. Roll out to fit a shallow tart tin, gently
pricking the base of the pastry. Bake in a moderate
oven at 200° C for only 15 minutes. Beat the eggs
and egg yolks with the cream. Stir in the herbs and
seasoning. Pour carefully and slowly into the cooked
pastry case, and place the tart tin on a baking sheet.
Bake until the filling is set and serve it hot. It's
much nicer that way.

INGREDIENTS

6 oz plain flour
1 egg yolk, twirled into
1 teaspoon milk
2 egg yolks
Seasoning
2 oz butter
2 eggs
2 oz mixed fresh parsley
  and chives, well chopped
¼ pint single Devonshire
  cream

A la Ronde can be found in Summer Lane, Exmouth, now a National Trust House, built in the eighteenth century. Two spinster cousins, Jane and Mary Parminter, on their return from a grand tour of Europe determined to embark on a unique house and to fill it with a fascinating collection of objects, some brought back from their travels. It was completed in 1796. A feather frieze and a shell-encrusted gallery, both so fragile they can only be viewed on closed-circuit television, are but two of an array of unique *objets de vertu*.

This '*A la Ronde*' House at Exmouth is decorated inside with shells and feathers. This pleasant Devon town with its 2-mile-long seafront stretches from the Docks to the red sandstone cliffs at Orcombe Point. In 1792 Exmouth started to develop into a seaside resort and its Georgian houses, a terrace called the Beacon, and a wide Esplanade, plus a mild climate, assured its success.

Killerton Pork Hot Pot

METHOD

Brown the meat in the melted lard for 5 minutes. Add the onion, cooking for a further 5 minutes. Chop in the tomato and add stock and seasoning. Cover the pan and simmer on the fire for another hour and a half, then serve with coarse rye bread. Some additional stock may need to be added during the cooking.

The measure of cream suggested at the end of the cooking time we thought had crept in over the years unsuitable to so rich and heavy a meat. We preferred one teaspoonful of dried marjoram stirred in just before serving.

This could well have been derived from an original 'cauldron' days recipe.

INGREDIENTS

2 oz lard
1½ lb pork shoulder, cut up
12 oz sliced onions
1 large tomato
A little ground sea salt and pepper
8 fl. oz stock

Chicken and Leek Cobbler

METHOD

Preheat oven to 200° C. Core and cut the apple into cubes. Heat oil and chicken in a pan. Add chopped leek and apple. Cook for a few minutes, then add cider. Crumble the stock cube into 150 ml water and add to the rest. Simmer over gentle heat. Place flour in a bowl, add cubed butter and rub together until the mixture looks like breadcrumbs. Grate the cheese and stir half into the mixture. Add the milk to make the dough. Roll out 2 cm thickness. Cut out scones with a round cutter. Put chicken mix in a casserole. Top with the scones brushed with a little milk. Sprinkle with the rest of the cheese and cook in a moderate oven for 25 minutes.

INGREDIENTS

2 chicken breasts
1 leek
1 apple
1 teaspoon sunflower oil
150 ml cider
1 chicken stock cube
3 ½ oz self-raising flour
1 oz butter
1 oz cheddar cheese
85 ml skimmed milk

The county, like so many others, still harks back to the old beliefs relating to food. Amongst so many taboos, the pot should never be stirred 'widdershins' (the direction of the witches' circular dance). Follow the direction of the sun. Never throw egg shells on the fire or your hens will stop laying, and above all, bread being the 'staff of life', to ensure dough rises on baking day mark all loaves with a cross on top to drive out the Devil. The belief in the power of witches to spoil food and turn milk sour lasted into the twentieth century in some parts.

Badgworthy Water in the Doone Valley. In the romantic story of *Lorna Doone*, Tom Faggus, the highwayman with the strawberry mare Winnie, led an existence tantamount to that of Dick Turpin and Black Bess, another wonder horse. The lonely valley of Badgworthy Water in Doone Valley was their territory. 'Everybody cursed the Doones but good people liked Mr Faggus. Ostlers and stable boys worshipped him.'

Tavistock Beef with Dumplings

METHOD

Mix the flour, salt and pepper together and roll the beef cubes in the flour mixture. Heat the butter and brown the onion and beef cubes in it. Remove with a slatted spoon, placing meat and onions in a large, oven-proof casserole. Then pour in the cider, beef stock, bay leaf. Cover casserole and cook in a moderate oven for 2 hours.

METHOD

Put all in a mixing bowl, but add the water carefully. The dumpling mixture should not be soggy. Shape into small balls on a floured board and put in casserole 30 minutes before cooking time ends. Finally spoon over the cream just before serving. It looks mouth-watering brought to the table with a large ladle and lots of fresh crusty bread.

INGREDIENTS

2 lb stewing beef, cubed, all fat removed
1 large Spanish onion
2 pints home-made beef stock
4 tablespoons flour
1 cup cream
1 teaspoon black pepper
1 teaspoon salt
3 oz butter
2 tablespoons cider
1 bay leaf

THE DUMPLINGS

2 beaten free-range eggs
4 tablespoons water
2 tablespoons chopped, fresh parsley
8 oz breadcrumbs
Seasoning
1 grated onion

Tavistock is close to Plymouth but street names are reminiscent of London because the Dukes of Bedford had Devonshire possessions and those of Bloomsbury, London, as well, plus such titles as Marquis of Tavistock. The discovery of copper in the Devon area led to a mining boom and as early as 1281 Tavistock was a Stannary Town (an official centre) for assaying tin, and a source of wealth.

The drinking fountain for horses was dry in the hot summer of 1976 when last we visited Bere Ferrers near Tavistock, but this one is lush with the ferns that grow so well in Devon along with magnolias, primroses, celandine, bluebells, wood anemones and ragged robin. All the way to Bere Ferrers, lanes wind and plunge over mossy bridges and stonework like this, covered with algae and lichen that has taken years to grow.

Devon Roast Lamb

METHOD
Peel and slice the potatoes. Put the sliced potatoes and onions into a roasting tin. Put in the stock. Place the lamb on top, scattering with seasoning and the rosemary and put into a hot oven. Cook for 2 hours, lowering oven temperature towards the end of cooking, by which time some evaporation has allowed the potato tops to brown and the meat juices to flavour the vegetables. It is best to trim off any surplus fat from the joint before cooking.

INGREDIENTS

Shoulder of lamb
1 lb potatoes
1 pint lamb stock
3 small onions, sliced
Seasoning
1 teaspoon chopped rosemary

Bellever Bridge on the River Dart – a post bridge.

Kingsteignton has a Ram Roasting Fair on spring bank holiday Monday based on a happening centuries ago. The stream that flowed through the churchyard and village suddenly dried up, only to reappear when a ram was sacrificed, so the custom continues.

An area once forested; The Lawn, Sidmouth. Verderers in the South West of England might also in some cases be petty constables. A verderer was an officer responsible for the king's forest. The post, held for life, dates back to the eleventh century. There were four to each forest who attended the Court of Attachment every forty days and punished minor offences. There were also wood-reeves or forest-keepers. Horse-shoe-shaped groups of stones with the open end facing a stream were called deer roasts and were used for cooking venison when it became permissible in some cases to shoot or cull deer.

Clovelly Meat Pasty

METHOD

Make the pastry and roll out to about ¼ inch thick. Cut into rounds using a saucer or small plate. Cut up the meat into small pieces, rejecting anything inedible such as gristle, lumps of fat or bone. Dice the raw potato and finely chop the onion. Mix the meat, onion and potato together very thoroughly, all salt and pepper and about 3 tablespoons of cold water. Place some of this filling on one half of each circle of pastry, damp the edges of the latter with cold water and fold over to cover the mixture. Press the edges of the pastry together and crimp it with the fingers to seal. Make two or three ventilating slits in the 'lid', brush with beaten egg or milk if a glaze is required and place on a baking tray. Cook in a hot oven at 200° C until the pastry is pale brown, then reduce the heat to 180° C for about 40 minutes.

INGREDIENTS

1 lb shortcrust pastry
12 oz raw mutton or steak
Seasoning
6 oz potatoes
1 small onion
3 tablespoons cold water

Mary Hobbs of Clovelly still makes traditional herb pasties, and young Michelle Luke, also of Clovelly, told us of her grandmother's Taty Pastries, the filling of which consists of sliced potatoes and cream.

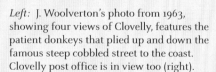

Above: The New Inn, Clovelly, was known for seafood and cider in the 1920s when this photograph was taken. It shows the familiar Clovelly sight of patient donkeys traversing the cobbled High Street. With their basketwork panniers, they have done so over a hundred years, usually attended by a fisherman.

Left: J. Woolverton's photo from 1963, showing four views of Clovelly, features the patient donkeys that plied up and down the famous steep cobbled street to the coast. Clovelly post office is in view too (right).

Lynton Herb Pasty

METHOD

Chop and scald a quantity of well-washed parsley, watercress or spinach. Cut up finely some shallots or leeks and one or two rashers of bacon. Place the vegetables and bacon on rounds of shortcrust pastry (as for Meat Pasty), crimp each pasty except at one point, and pour into this a small amount of beaten egg. Seal the pasties and bake as usual.

Meat or herb pasties would be excellent fare for a train journey and hotels like Lyndale and Tors Park, both at Lynmouth, used to put up picnic hampers for visitors.

Above: Lynmouth, the quay, around 1924. Closely linked Lynmouth and Lynton came into the news in 1812 when poet Percy Bysshe Shelley and his sixteen-year-old bride, Mary Wollstoncraft, eloped and hid away in Lynmouth, much to the anger of Mary's parents, but front-page news erupted in August 1952 when a cloudburst fell on Exmoor and East and West Lyn rivers raged, sweeping cars and buildings into the sea. Thirty-four people died.

Right: The Lynton & Lynmouth Cliff Railway was sponsored to link the two after the construction of the narrow gauge railway from Barnstaple to Lynton, which operated from 1898–1935. The Cliff Railway is water-powered as it makes its precipitous descent, the two carriages being counter-balanced by 700-gallon water tanks.

The 1895 *Ward Lock & Bowden's Guide to Torquay and Dartmouth* advertised the Lynton, Lynmouth and Barnstaple fast four-horse coach *Tantivy*. 'Carrying the mails, it runs daily through the year (Sundays excepted).' Additional coaches during the summer season were *Glen Lyn* and *Tally Ho*, all fast four-horse coaches of Messrs Jones Bros. The 3.21 train from Barnstaple Junction brought passengers to Waterloo, London in seven hours once the *Tantivy* had deposited them at the railway station.

The Tors Park Hotel, under Cecil H. Bevan, advertised 20 miles of trout and salmon fishing, 2,000 acres of shooting, and the only tennis court in Lymouth. The Devon and Somerset Foxhounds met 'within easy distance of the hotel'.

Exeter Early Summer Hotch Potch

METHOD

The young vegetables should be washed, carrots and turnips cut small, lettuce pulled apart leaf by leaf and the shallot onions chopped well, including the green tops. Put all, with parsley and thyme, into the good mutton stock and simmer for ½ hour. Then add the peas and the washed white part of cauliflower, broken into small, dainty springs. Simmer on until these also are cooked. The whole process takes about one hour. Season towards the end. The old way was also to put leftover meat from the joint, a few minutes before serving, into the hotch potch, but it is not now considered advisable to warm up meat in this way. The young vegetables are a wonderful treat in themselves.

INGREDIENTS

1 quart good mutton stock
6 spring onions
2 young turnips
1 cup freshly shelled peas
1 lettuce (cabbage shaped)
4 young carrots
1 small cauliflower
1 sprig each of fresh parsley and thyme

We ate a simple but excellent soup at The Spinney, Shirwell, prepared by Janet Pelling, based on a rich bone stock with an assortment of autumn vegetables. A scattering of fresh parsley on each portion added more subtle flavour.

Left: Drawing by C. Russell of the Guildhall, Exeter. Exeter Old High Street shows one example of its ancient buildings, this one captured in 1909. A plaque marks the spot where one timber-framed Tudor building stood, but which, because it was in the way of a new road, had to be jacked up and rolled to a new site. A display of the world-famous Honiton lace, which Queen Victoria and royal babies wore, is on show in Exeter's museum.

Below: The High Street, Honiton, Devon, 1932. A town famous for beautiful lace, which can be seen on display in Exeter.

THE GUILDHALL, EXETER

Sandy Bay, Combe Martin Rabbit with Cream

METHOD

Wipe and joint the rabbit, rolling the joints in the seasoned flour. Heat the butter and toss the chopped celery into it. Cook gently for 5 minutes. Place in a casserole, then brown the rabbit in the butter with the onions. Put these also into the casserole, season, and pour in the cider, the bunch of herbs and the cream. Cook in a moderate oven until the rabbit is tender. It takes about 2 hours.

In Devon, small balls made of sage and onion stuffing with chopped bacon are sometimes served with the rabbit.

INGREDIENTS

1 rabbit
1 chopped celery heart
½ pint cider
Bunch of herbs
2 oz butter
1 medium chopped onion
¼ pint cream
Seasoned flour

Newberry Beach and Sandy Bay, Combe Martin, 1952.

Sidmouth Devonshire Brawn

METHOD

All the meat must be thoroughly scalded and put into a stew pot. Cover with cold water and bring to the boil. After skimming, simmer on for 2 hours until the meat is falling from the bones. Remove the bones and cut the meat up, removing any fat and allowing to go cold. The meat is now jellied and should be put back into the stew pot. Put on gentle heat; season with salt, pepper and mace. Simmer on for 10 minutes then turn into a mould and leave to set. Do not cut into it until quite cold.

INGREDIENTS

1 pig's cheek
3 large trotters
Seasoning
1 pig's ear
1 tongue
Pinch of powdered mace

Devonshire rabbit or pig's brawn was always accompanied with mustard, the brawn cut into thick slices, the English mustard mixed with cream. I am told that rabbit brawn was also traditional in Devon but the boar, and later its descendant the pig, especially at Christmas time, seems to have been the norm.

The old forge at Branscombe near Sidmouth seems as 'Heavenly Devonly' as the show village of Cockington, Devon, where Rose Cottage sells Devon violet perfume and has one Ye Olde Wishing Well, but both places are genuinely beautiful. At Ash Farm dairy we heard about clotted cream from Jessie Hewer and collected recipes for Country Venison Pie and Cider Fruitcake.

Dartmouth Pie

METHOD

Put 2 of the chops in a deep pie dish, then a layer of apples sprinkled with seasoning, sugar and spice. Next lay slices of onion. Repeat this, seasoning as you go. Pour in the cider. Make a fairly thick pastry crust to cover the pie dish. To allow steam to escape, make a hole in the top. Brush with egg yolk and milk whisked together and bake in a moderate oven for 1¼ hours. Some people add cream but this is rather too rich with pork.

INGREDIENTS

8 oz shortcrust pastry
4 boned chops of pork, with fat removed
Freshly ground pepper and salt
2 peeled, sliced onions
Pinch of nutmeg
1 pint cider
4 large apples, cored, peeled and sliced

Dartmouth. These photographs from 1920 shows Dartmouth Castle and St Petrov's church. The castle changed hands twice during the Civil War between King Charles I and Parliament. A famous citizen was Thomas Newcomen, an ironmonger who in 1811 designed what is thought to be the oldest working steam engine in the world. The engine was brought to Dartmouth to celebrate Thomas's 300th anniversary. Dartmouth Castle overlooks the estuary of the River Dart.

Harvest home suppers were occasions of rejoicing, involving a good spread of country food, songs sung, toasts to the master and mistress, then dancing to the fiddle. Reading about the faggers' or farmworkers' supper, which preceded harvest home and was prepared for gangs of itinerant farmworkers, it seems that meat and herb pasties, boiled hams, roasted fowls, bowls of baked potatoes washed down with beer and cider were set on the table at 7 o'clock in the evening. At 9 o'clock 'we did give them more to eat and filled their muggs and did pay them for their work, and did give each a handful of baccy'.

Two days later followed the real harvest home: '6 bigge fowls, 3 hares, 2 gret bigge hams and a bakin chine … tartes, custards and other swete things'. Drinks consisted of beer, cider, brandy, wines, 'with milk and lemmon water for the youngsters'.

If a cow had calved, beastings were available to make rich puddings. Only of interest today as a recipe from long ago, the 'beastinges' were strained, sugar, muscatel raisins and currants added, cinnamon dusted on top, then they were baked 'for nearly two howers by the clocke'. It must have been a very slow oven to prevent curdling.

Our last trip into Devon was at harvest time. Markets everywhere had splendid displays of fruit and vegetables, amongst the latter, healthy looking kale, cauliflowers, kohlrabi, cabbage and broccoli plus a great selection of fresh herbs, honey and cheeses. Thoughts and conversation turned to the harvest suppers of a century and more ago 'when cut and come again was the order of the evening'. Passed down memories from by-standing Devonians: 'buckets of taties mashed with lard and cabbage'; 'beer, cider and frothing horns of ale', but first the celebrating harvesters lifted the neck of corn dressed with gay ribbons and set it on the mantelpiece. Bacon and peas were cooked with a saddle of mutton and sausages. 'Plum pudding was placed on pewter plates with the mutton.' Harvest songs were sung and much raising of pots and tankards as farmers and villagers roared, 'The corn, oh, the corn, 'tis the ripening of corn …' Mincemeat in those days was made from golden pippin apples finely shredded, with spices, vine fruits and finely shredded undercut of sirloin of beef.

In a Devon courtyard, reminiscent of Cadhay, Totnes townspeople proceed to the Guildhall. Wearing Elizabethan dress, this procession enhances historical interest each Tuesday from June to September in a town dating back to the Saxon era. Trips on the river are available and lively markets every Tuesday and Friday.

Haunch of Venison

After being hung, the venison should be allowed to marinate for three days, turning gently.

METHOD
The prepared haunch is spread with melted butter and well sprinkled with salt and pepper. Make a flour and water paste and roll it out after kneading it well. It must be big enough to cover the haunch of venison. Bake it in a moderate oven for 3 hours. The timing depends on size. After this peel off the hardened paste and return the joint to a hot oven to brown. The paste prevents undue drying out of the flesh, which tends to dryness.

My grandmother used to cook venison in a terracotta lidded pot, with trotters.

THE MARINADE

1 pint vinegar
3 pints red wine
1 bay leaf
1 medium-sized sliced onion
½ pint olive oil
1 clove of garlic
A few cloves

Hayes Barton, the birthplace of Sir Walter Raleigh.

The National Park at Exmoor has the largest wild herd of red deer outside Scotland.

Exmouth in the sixteenth century was very important and used as a base by Sir Walter Raleigh. The clock tower was a gift to the town from the Lord of the Manor, Mark Rolle, on the occasion of Queen Victoria's Diamond Jubilee. A favourite eighteenth-century Georgian town, its mild air was recommended for invalids.

Bristol Mamble Lamb Pipkin

METHOD

'In a fireproof pipkin place cubed neck end of lamb or mutton with fat removed, add 2 chopped courgettes, a small handful of sultanas, a tablespoon of washed rice, ¼ lb shelled peas. Cook in cider or wine. On the top place a thick layer of sliced potatoes as in hot pot.'

These are directions from a busy chef. The lamb keeps very hot in this traditional cooking pot, and the wine and sultanas make it rather special. Cooking time is about 1¾ hours on 190° C. A little basting of the potato topping with butter makes them brown, or you can simply shake the pipkin gently 30 minutes before cooking time finishes. The juices overrunning the potatoes brown them nicely.

One of our calling places *en route* to Devon was Bristol, where we had the mysteriously named but delicious Mamble Lamb.

Left: The Victoria Rooms, Bristol, with its spectacular fountain in 1930. A famous seafaring city, in the Middle Ages, Bristol was a cloth exporting port, its chief import being wine. John and Sebastian Cabot sailed from here on their great voyage of discovery. Bristol has five museums and an art gallery. Every day it holds a fish market.

Brixham Tomato Relish

METHOD

Skin and chop tomatoes. Peel and chop onions and place all in a pan with rest of ingredients. Heat gently at first, the simmer steadily until it thickens, which takes 1½ hours. Pot.

INGREDIENTS

3 lb tomatoes
1 lb onions
1 teaspoon finely ground sea salt
½ pint malt vinegar
8 oz brown sugar

Apple Chutney

METHOD

Peel, core and chop apples. Peel and chop onion. Place together with the rest of the ingredients in a stainless steel pan. Let the sugar dissolve slowly then cook on until mushy, about 1½ hours, by which time the chutney will have thickened and be ready for potting.

INGREDIENTS

1 lb Bramley apples
½ lb seedless raisins
1 teaspoon sea salt
¼ teaspoon allspice
1 lb brown sugar
1 onion
¼ teaspoon nutmeg
1 pint malt vinegar

Apple and Sultana Chutney

METHOD

Place the malt vinegar in a stainless steel pan. Add brown sugar, sultanas and apples. Prepare a muslin bag containing the ginger and spice. Boil all on low heat for almost 2 hours, remove the muslin bag and discard. Pot the chutney in heated jars and cover securely.

INGREDIENTS

1½ pints malt vinegar
1 ½ lb brown sugar
1 lb washed sultanas
2 lb Bramley apples, peeled cored and chopped
1 oz bruised root ginger
1 oz pickling spice

Cakes, Puddings, Pies

In the nineteenth century, cooks were urged to use Brownhill's Feculina for sponge cakes, seed, sultana, snow cakes and raspberry sandwiches, also rich plum puddings. Brownhill's also made table jellies which they claimed were 'pure and strengthening'.

An 1870 advertisement lists all their jellies: lemon, raspberry, blackcurrant, strawberry, port wine, cherry calve's foot (for invalids) and damson.

Totnes Blackberry and Apple Flummery

METHOD

Clean and pick the blackberries and peel and core the apples. Stew the fruit in water, sweeten to taste and press through a sieve. Mix the flour and spice to a smooth liquid with a little cold water. Boil the fruit purée and pour it on the flour, stirring well. Return the mixture to the pan and stir till it boils. Boil for 5 minutes and when cool enough, pour into a glass dish. When cold, serve with double cream. Raspberries, redcurrants or blackcurrants also made a good flummery. Serve on a hot day and don't use anything other than double cream.

INGREDIENTS

1 lb blackberries
½ pint water
½ teaspoon mixed spice
1 lb apples
2 oz flour
sugar to taste

Close to Totnes is a very ancient village called Rattery, with thatched, whitewashed cottages and, anciently, it was famous or notorious for a special brew of ale. The Church House Inn was founded in the eleventh century.

Fig Flapjack

This flapjack emerges from the oven about 2 inches thick with its bottom layer of crumble, thick layer of mashed figs and dates, topped by more crumble, which is simply made.

METHOD
Cream butter and sugar then stir in oats. Press firmly into tin and bake at 150° C following directions above. The fig mixture consists of equal quantities of stewed figs and packet dates mashed together with a little golden syrup and a teaspoon of warm water. Cooking time is about 30 minutes.

INGREDIENTS

8 oz oats
4 oz demerara sugar
4 oz butter
Stewed figs and packet dates

Leftover pastry, as in so many counties, was not wasted but rolled out and filled or studded with dried fruits e.g. currants, raisins, chopped figs. Devon, Cornwall and Sussex pressed in raisins and currants, calling these baked morsels – which children loved – Plum Heavies.

Wholemeal Cottage Loaves

METHOD
Crush the vitamin C tablet amongst the sugar and place $\frac{1}{3}$ of the warm water into a bowl. Into this whisk the dried yeast and leave in a warm place. In a large mixing bowl place flour, salt and lard. Rub the fat into the flour, stir in the yeast mixture and mix all thoroughly with the flat of the hand. Turn the dough onto a floured surface and knead it well to work the yeast throughout. After 10 minutes' kneading divide the dough into 2 large pieces and 2 smaller. Making traditional cottage loaves, place one above the other, the top half being the size of the base. Make a hole in the top which penetrates to the second layer. Cover loosely with greased polythene or a clean tea towel and leave to rise for 30 minutes. Bake at 230° C in a preheated oven for 35 minutes. This makes 2 cottage loaves. Bread that is correctly baked sounds hollow when the base of the loaf is tapped by the knuckles. The addition of vitamin C to an old recipe obviates the need for lengthy proving by strengthening the gluten.

INGREDIENTS

3 lb stone-ground whole-wheat flour
1 oz lard
1 tablespoon brown sugar
1¾ pints warm water
1 oz dried yeast
1 tablespoon salt
1 crushed vitamin C tablet

Lancashire was once famous for its Sad Cake, bursting with sugar and currants (moistened sometimes with 'fiery water' (brandy) but usually water). Only the old fire ovens can cook this to perfection.

Visitors in *Lorna Doone* country look out for Oare Manor and Oare Church, the latter famous for the scene of John Ridd and Lorna Doone's wedding. The window at which Carver Doone shot at Lorna is still there and there is a bust of R. D. Blackmore commemorating the centenary of his birth in 1825. Exmoor became his playground as a boy. He knew it so well and I loved his story. It was my first school prize.

Left: The window from where Carver Doone shot Lorna Doone.

Below: Oare Church, where Lorna Doone and John Ridd were married.

Ginger Snaps

METHOD
Rub the butter into the flour, add the sugar and
ginger, then mix in the syrup and honey. The soda
dissolved in hot water should be tipped in last and
quickly. Roll out, cut into biscuits, and bake in a
moderate oven for 15 minutes.

INGREDIENTS

½ lb flour
¼ lb brown sugar
½ oz ground ginger
1 level saltspoon
bicarbonate of
soda dissolved in 1
tablespoon of hot water
Large nut of butter
1 tablespoon clear honey
2 tablespoons syrup

These are biscuits that came from Shaldon, where
the postmistress kindly showed me round on her
day off, the best way because she knew it so well.
I recall the fine view of a distant Torquay we had
from a high point, beneath which lay Smugglers'
Tunnel, cut by Lord Clifford. Thereby hangs a tale of smugglers
but his Lordship only wanted to reach his beach (private) for daily swims.

Appledore Apple Amber

METHOD
Peel, core, cut up the apples and stew them with the
sugar and water until they fall. Mash them well with
a wooden spoon and add the butter. Separate whites
of eggs from yolks. Break up yolks and stir into the
fruit mixture. Line the sides of the pie dish with a
strip of pastry, crimping the edges. Pour in the fruit.
Beat the whites of the eggs stiffly, then mix in the
ounce of caster sugar and pile it on top of the fruit.
Bake in a hot oven for only 20 minutes.

METHOD
Rub the soft margarine or butter into the flour
and bind with a little water. Roll out quickly and
lightly, keeping everything cool.

INGREDIENTS

4 oz short pastry
4 oz demerara sugar
2 oz butter
½ cup water
1½ lb apples
2 eggs
1 oz caster sugar

THE SHORTCRUST
PASTRY

4 oz soft margarine or
butter
8 oz flour

All Devon seems proud of Sir Francis Drake, and a shipyard in Appledore built a full-scale model of Drake's flagship, the *Golden Hind*, which like its original has also sailed round the world. I cannot be sure, but I think we saw it once in Brixham harbour.

Westward Ho! Coffee Marshmallow Whip

This is a Second World War recipe from Torquay.

METHOD
Put the marshmallows, cut in small pieces, in the top of a double boiler. Pour over them the coffee, thoroughly strained. Stir over flame until the marshmallows are quite soft; pour mixture into a bowl and whisk until frothy. Divide into glasses and, when cool, pour over a little whipped cream and sprinkle with chopped nuts. Place in refrigerator until needed.

INGREDIENTS
½ lb marshmallows
1 cup strong coffee

Westward Ho!, founded in 1863, was named after Charles Kinsgley's novel about seafarers in the days of Elizabeth I. Kiplings Tor at Westward Ho! also remembers Rudyard Kipling, the author of *Stalky and Co.* because he attended the college there and his book is about college life. Gorse, shingle and sand dunes dominate the scenery, with its caravan sites and holiday camps.

Torridge House at Westward Ho!

West Country Tart

METHOD

Line a greased dish with shortcrust pastry. Beat the
eggs together with the gently warmed syrup, sugar
and walnuts. The filling should then be put in the
pastry case and baked in a moderate oven for ½
hour. Traditionally, this tart was also served with
cream.

In testing, I used a scatter of fine shortbread
mixture on top of the filling. This made the sweet
filling less likely to brown and burn round the
edges.

A treacle tart from Simonsbath was an
alternative – 'Line a shallow, buttered dish with shortcrust pastry. Put
in 3 tablespoons of treacle then scatter on 3 oz of fine breadcrumbs. Sprinkle with
lemon juice and bake for 20 minutes in a hot oven.' The old pastry recipes mainly
used lard for shortcrust: 4 oz rubbed lightly into 8 oz of flour until 'crumbled' then
bound with a little iced water.

INGREDIENTS

6 oz shortcrust pastry
1 oz brown sugar, well
   pounded
2 eggs
8 oz golden syrup
3 oz finely chopped
   walnuts

The Jary Mews and Coaching Establishment, run by J. Truscott, Job Master, organised trips over
Dartmoor in connection with the Great Western Railway Company's trains – 'carriages, wagonettes,
charabancs always on hire'. In 1929 most converged on Dartmoor's accessible spots, for visitors
were anxious to include this vast, romantic area of bogs and tors in their itineraries just as they
were to descant on the rugged coast at Labrador, Torquay.

Bideford Fruit Flapjacks

METHOD
Melt the butter and honey gently in a pan. Stir in the sultanas and cherries, then the oats, mixing well together. Press the mixture into a well-greased tin and bake in a moderate oven for half an hour. Cut the flapjack into squares when it has cooled a little and remove from tin, otherwise it is difficult to get out.

This is another recipe from the late Josephine Houghton, who lived later at Crownhill Road, Plymouth.

INGREDIENTS

4 oz honey
3 oz butter
2 oz sultanas
6 oz rolled oats
1 oz glacé cherries or figs, chopped

Pete Wright's mighty traction engine from Bideford, seen on display with other monsters in 1984. Once a busy port, trading from the long quay at Bideford stretched as far off as Spain, the West Indies and North America. Sea Captain Sir Richard Greville is the town's famous son. He died in 1591 fighting fifteen Spanish Galleons off the Azores.

Devon Flaky Pastry

METHOD
Sieve flour and salt into a mixing bowl. Cut half of the hardened lard into 'chippings' and mix into the flour. Add the water very gradually to make dough, i.e. pastry. Roll out and add the remainder of the lard in small quantities all over the rolled out pastry. Fold over at least 8 times, roll out, fold again and roll out. Chill the pastry in a fridge and make a lid for your fruit pie.

INGREDIENTS

8 oz plain flour
8 oz lard
4 tablespoons cold water
Pinch of salt

At the Quince Honey Farm, South Molton, where we stopped for Devon honey, wild colonies and unique observation hives behind glass can be watched in safety. It is acknowledged to be the world's best honeybee exhibition.

Teignmouth Honey Cake

METHOD
Sift the flour and pour the warmed honey and butter into the well of flour mix. Add the beaten eggs and beat all the mixture well together. Bake in a buttered tin for one hour at 125° C.

INGREDIENTS

8 oz flour
3 oz Devon honey
6 oz butter
2 eggs

Teignmouth and Dawlish have a well-known railway tunnel running between them in which the famous Victorian engineer Isambard Kingdom Brunel had a hand. This section of the Great Western Railway proved to be a great feat of engineering. The scenery here is stunning and dramatic, especially if the weather is wild, for the sea can dash over the trains.

The coast of Labrador near Teignmouth was depicted in 1930 in a hand-coloured souvenir postcard costing three half-pence to send.

The long bridge connecting the north bank of the estuary at Teignmouth to the small village of Shaldon near the Ness was built in 1826 by engineer Robert Hopkins. After twelve years it was in a parlous state, brought about by ship worm boring into its piles. Arches gave way and it had to be closed for repairs, completed 1840.

The beach at Shaldon used to abound in shells. At the garden at Labrador strawberry teas were specially prepared for visitors, whose trip was usually completed by crossing the river on ferry boat, then returning by wagonette to Torquay.

A beautiful 1902 postcard of Teignmouth, which was originally a Saxon town. From its quay built in the 1830s Dartmouth granite was shipped to build London Bridge, the one which was later shipped to the United States and now spans a man-made waterway in Arizona. John Keats stayed here while writing his poem 'Endymion'.

The Ness and Lighthouse at Teignmouth in the early 1920s.

Shaldon Apple Pie and Clotted Cream (also found at Sidmouth)

METHOD

Butter a deep enamelled plate and line it with the shortcrust pastry. Mix together the cinnamon, sugar and grated lemon rind. Peel, core and slice the apples, arranging the slices in layers with the cinnamon, sugar and rind between the layers. Pour over this the melted butter. Cover with a pastry lid, pinching the edges of the pastry all round the plate, together to seal. Make a slit in the top and bake for ¾ hour in a fairly hot oven. Traditionally served all over Devon with clotted cream (not cheese as in my native Lancashire).

INGREDIENTS

1 lb cooking apples
Grated rind of half a lemon
Pinch of cinnamon
4 oz caster sugar
1 oz butter
½ lb shortcrust pastry

At Marldon in Devon the Apple Pie Fair takes place at the beginning of August. Founded in 1888, it lapsed during the First World War, but was revived in 1958. Under a large pie crust, large quantities of apples are baked and the pie dragged to the fairground by a donkey, where portions are sold. The ceremony originated from the days when poor farm labourers relied on windfalls of apples to supplement their families' diet. Long ago Marldon decided to bake one big pie in the communal bakehouse and have a village party. Other counties traditionally do likewise, using meat or other fruits to fill the hefty pie.

In January 1811 an 'extraordinary large cake', 18 foot in circumference and half a ton in weight could be viewed at 41 Cheapside, London, and was to celebrate Twelfth Night after Christmas. Portions were ordered and sent all over the country.

A typical Devon cottage at Sidmouth, photographed in 1950.

Salcombe Regis Cheese Scones

METHOD

Place flour, baking powder and mustard into a bowl and rub in the butter till the mixture resembles fine breadcrumbs. Stir in the cheese and yoghurt and milk to make a soft dough. Turn onto a floured surface, knead gently and roll into a circle about ¾ inch thick. On a baking tray lightly greased with butter, cut into wedges and brush with beaten egg and a scatter of grated cheese. Bake on 220° C for 20 minutes. Best eaten warm with butter or can accompany a savoury dish.

INGREDIENTS

8 oz self-raising wholemeal flour
1 teaspoon baking powder
1 teaspoon dry mustard
1 oz butter
2 oz Cheddar cheese, grated
¼ pint natural yoghurt
2 tablespoons milk

Date and Rice Pudding

METHOD

Wash the rice and stream it into a saucepan of boiling water. Boil for 15 minutes. Strain. Put the rice into a pie dish. Mix with it the honey and well-chopped dates. Beat the egg and milk. Stir this in and bake in a slow oven.

INGREDIENTS

1 tablespoon honey
8 oz dates, washed, stoned
2 tablespoons rice
1 egg
¾ pint milk

Sidbury has the Old Bakery and delightful shops selling cakes, honey, clotted cream and Devonshire teas in premises of thatch, whitewashed cob and slate, and it is not far from Axminster, with its grand eighteenth-century George Hotel.

Paignton Carrot Cake

METHOD

Preheat oven to 180° C. Grease an 8-inch square tin. Put butter, sugar, yoghurt, flour, baking powder and eggs in a mixing bowl and beat together. Then fold in 2 oz of the nuts, grated carrot, orange zest and cinnamon, mixing well into a smooth dough. Put mixture into the tin and smooth the surface. Bake in the centre of the oven for 30–40 minutes. When cool take the carrot cake out of the tin gently by running a knife round it to loosen and transfer it to a wire tray.

A topping of 4 oz soft cheese, 4 tablespoons icing sugar and the grated zest of one lemon, all mixed well together, can be smoothed over the cooled carrot cake and finished off with a few more nuts if desired to produce a 'party cake', but the basic recipe is the old Devon way.

INGREDIENTS

2 ½ oz soft butter
3 ½ oz light Muscovado sugar
3 tablespoons natural yoghurt
7 oz wholemeal self-raising flour
1 teaspoon baking powder
2 eggs, well beaten
2 ½ oz hazelnuts
6 oz carrots, finely grated
Zest of 1 orange, finely grated
1 teaspoon ground cinnamon

Paignton, Torquay's neighbour, had an advantage over the premier south-west-facing holiday town in its plentiful sands, which stretch northwards for 1 mile to Hollicombe Head. Although a suburb of Torquay, it is an ancient town, connected 100 years ago with a frequent service of steam launches. The ruins of the Bishop's Palace of Exeter and the Church of St John are to be found here. By the 1890s a promenade, pier and esplanade had been made. Paignton was visited in spring for the sight of the apple orchards in full bloom, cider being manufactured on a large scale.

The Windsor Wooley Girls from Poulton-le-Fylde around 1931, dancing before a crowded summertime audience in their tour of the South Coast. Judging by the size of the audience this may be Torquay or Paignton. The days of Panama hats.

Arlington Court Snow Pancakes

METHOD
The method is to mix the flour into the milk by slow degrees (to sieve it in). Beat in the egg and add the snow last, just before frying. A thick frying pan is best with the fat very hot so take care to prevent splattering, work slowly and gradually, a few minutes on both sides is enough, then stack each pancake, separating them with a sprinkle of sugar. Keep them warm and serve with real lemon juice. The snow makes wonderfully light pancakes.

INGREDIENTS

3 tablespoons flour
3 tablespoons snow
1 egg
Lard for frying
½ pint milk fresh from
   the cow

At Arlington Court the National Trust manageress said the Sunday roast was still popular in the restaurant but almost half of her customers preferred vegetarian dishes such as leeks in a cream cheese sauce and plenty of ground hazelnuts and almonds as topping.

Rules from the servants' hall of such great houses as Arlington make amusing reading: 'If anyone is observed wiping their knives on the table cloth at any time – forfeit 3 pence. All stable and other persons to come to dinner with their coats on.'

Snow in Devon – very unusual! It must have been a February about 1946 – artistic work by real children and a real chance to make Snow Pancakes. See recipe.

Magnolia in May at Arlington Court, noted for lichens, a heronry, and a colony of horseshoe bats; May being the best time to view the bats roosting in the roof of the house.

Torquay Caramel Peaches

METHOD

Skin the peaches by dipping them into boiling water
for 2 minutes. Cut in halves and remove stones. Fill
the centres with whipped cream. Join the halves
together, securing with thin sticks. Place brown
sugar, milk and butter in a saucepan. Stir until
boiling. Simmer for 8 minutes. Beat until it begins
to thicken then pour over the peaches. When cold,
slide out the sticks. Top each peach with a swirl of
cream and chopped almonds. These were often
accompanied by sponge biscuits.

INGREDIENTS

5 peaches
1 breakfast cup brown
    sugar
1 tablespoon butter
¼ pint whipped cream
2 tablespoons milk
1 tablespoon chopped nuts

Above: Princess
Promenade, Torquay, 1929.

Left: The tropical gardens
and seafront, Torquay.
'Dear Ma, I arrived safely
this morning. Jessue was at
the station to meet me' – a
postcard to Lytham in 1908
when Dorothy Gurney's
poem was popular in
Torquay. 'Oh, the little maids
of Devon/they have skins
of milk and cream/but who
looks at them is holden/with
the magic of a dream.'

Princess Pier and harbour in 1929 was a favourite promenading ground, with fine sea views to south and west. At the angle of the pier was the Concert Hall, where military bands played and entertainments by pierrots were given daily. Many types of seagoing craft were of interest to visitors. 'Every prospect pleases' was Torquay's slogan; Vane Hill, the Strand with its double row of trees, and Waldon Hill with Princess Gardens at its foot. St John's church contained frescoes and two paintings by the famous Victorian artist Burne-Jones.

Torquay Tipsy Trifle

METHOD

Sandwich the split-open sponges with the jams and jelly. Put in sufficient ratafia biscuits to cover base of a large, glass trifle dish and sprinkle with the brandy. Arrange half the sponges on top of the ratafias, sprinkle with sherry and almonds. Arrange the other half of the sponges on top with the rest of the almonds and sherry. Press down lightly. Heat the milk and cream in a saucepan. Beat egg yolks and sugar together. Pour the heated milk and cream over them and cook in a double boiler until the resulting custard coats the back of a wooden spoon. When it has cooled, pour over the sponges in the trifle bowl and allow to rest all night. Decorate with toasted almonds and angelica next day. It does not really need any more cream, but some people indulge, especially at Christmas tea.

INGREDIENTS

8 trifle sponges
2 level tablespoons each home-made strawberry jam and plum jam
2 tablespoons brandy
1 oz flaked almonds
1 pint milk
6 egg yolks
Toasted almonds
Ratafia biscuits
2 level tablespoons orange jelly
6 tablespoons sherry
¼ pint thick cream
3 level tablespoons caster sugar

'Torquay for Sunshine' has been the town's slogan and it is indeed one of the best-known and loved of England's seaside resorts. In 1848 the Great Western Railway came and Torquay never looked back. The poet Lord Alfred Tennyson loved it and even Napoleon, viewing from afar, had glowing words. Places like Austey's Cove lay sheltered at the shore end of a ferny combe by high cliffs of brilliantly coloured limestone. 'Thomas's Wooden House' in the early days received visitors to hire pleasure boats and bathing machines. Over the door he wrote, 'Picnics supplied with hot water and tea at a nice little house down by the sea. Fresh crabs and lobsters every day, red mullet ... bathing machines for ladies are kept with towels and gowns all quite covered. Thomas is the man who supplies everything, and also teaches young people to swim.'

Plymouth Pier and Hoe

For generations a steamer trip was reckoned to be the high spot of holidays at the seaside. SS *Pioneer* would leave Torquay harbour to sail in Torbay, passing Teignmouth, Brixham, Paignton, a pleasant trip on a sunny day. In the 1870s they went as far as Bournemouth in the paddle steamers. By 1881, *Empress* was the first steamer to make the trip from Bournemouth to Torquay and back in one day, taking thirteen and a half hours. In August 1886 the *Bournemouth* set off alongside its smaller rival, *Empress*. On the return journey they encountered thick fog in West Bay. *Bournemouth* ran onto rocks but fortunately there was no loss of life.

Chudleigh Custard Pudding

METHOD

Place the slices of bread and butter and the sultanas at the bottom of a buttered dish. Beat the eggs with the sugar and pour the milk onto them. Pour gently over the bread, distributing evenly, and grate a little nutmeg over the top. This delicious pudding should be cooked in a very moderate oven until set, which takes about 40 minutes.

INGREDIENTS

2 eggs
1 oz sugar
3 thin slices bread and butter
1 pint milk
Nutmeg
2 oz sultanas

Chudleigh market town was almost completely destroyed by fire in 1897. Fortunately the ancient building, which housed Devon schoolboys from 1668, still stands. This grammar school was founded by John Pynsent. It is said that another John – Dryden – completed his successful translation of Virgil at Chudleigh, for which he was paid £1,200. The town, 10 miles from Exeter, still draws interested tourists to view the limestone heights and caves of Chudleigh Rocks.

A high-speed train flashes over Saltash Bridge, spanning the River Tamar. One of Isambard Kingdom Brunel's masterpieces, this iconic bridge seems to typify West Country holidays and Devon food. Completed 1859 it runs alongside the suspension bridge opened 102 years later, which replaced a ferry service dating back to the thirteenth century.

Devonshire Splits

METHOD

Sieve flour and salt into a warm bowl. Rub in butter.
Cream yeast and sugar, adding the warmed milk (not hot).
Make a well in the flour. Add the yeast and liquid, beating
well in to form a soft dough. Cover bowl and set in a
warm place until the dough has doubled. On a floured
board knead lightly then divide the dough into 6 pieces.
Knead each into a round shape and place the splits on
a floured baking tray until they have doubled in size
(about 15 minutes). Brush tops with milk and bake in
a hot oven for 20 minutes until brown and risen. They
should sound hollow when tapped underneath. Cool on a wire tray. Splits are
favourites for Devon teas, filled with home-made strawberry jam and clotted cream.

INGREDIENTS

½ lb plain flour
½ oz butter
1 teaspoon sugar
1 teaspoon salt
½ oz yeast
¼ pint warm milk

Lots of Devonshire Splits on sale in
the big marquee the day we arrived
at this vintage tractor and steamroller
exhibition. Devonshire crafts such as
pottery added to the interest.

Okehampton Raspberry Tartlets

METHOD

Place the washed fruit in a pan with the sugar and water.
Stew gently for 5 minutes. Strain the fruit and put it in
a basin, returning the syrup to the pan. Boil it until it
becomes a thick syrup, reducing by half. Line 15 deep
patty tins with shortcrust pastry and place a piece of
greaseproof paper filled with rice in each. Bake for 15
minutes in a hot oven. Remove the rice and paper and
when cool put a little of the fruit in each tartlet and
pour a spoonful of syrup over it. Served with clotted
cream heaped on each, these tartlets are delicious.

INGREDIENTS

¾ lb short pastry
1 lb sugar
1 gill cream
1 lb raspberries
½ gill water

Fore Street, Okehampton.

Newton Abbot's market place in 1913, affording a good view of well-laid stalls, was one of the most important, at the head of the River Teign. The railway's arrival in 1846 turned it into a busy nodal town. Only the fourteenth-century tower of St Leonard's church has survived as proof of the town's medieval past. A David Skipp watercolour.

Strawberries and clotted cream is everybody's favourite and our June/July trips to Devon leave happy memories of the 'Strawberry boys' alongside large signs on the busy roads, their barrows stacked high in the early morning, but empty boxes piled by evening.

Lee Apple Scone

METHOD
Preheat oven to 200° C. Sift flour, baking powder and
spice into a bowl. Rub in the butter till the mixture
resembles breadcrumbs. Stir in sugar. Peel, core
and grate the apple and mix it into the flour. Add a
very little milk to make a soft dough. Shape into a
round on a floured board and brush with milk. Bake
in oven for 25 minutes. Allow to cool, then split,
buttering thickly.

INGREDIENTS

8 oz wholemeal flour
¼ teaspoon cinnamon
2 oz brown sugar
Milk to mix and glaze
2 teaspoons baking
    powder
2 oz butter
8 oz cooking apples

The Old Maid's Cottage at Lee near Ilfracombe, photographed
by the Swiss Brothers of The Arcade in 1934. A favourite
rendezvous for cream teas here and at the George Hotel in
Lee Bay, reached from a well-wooded valley leading down to a
small cove, brightened with luxurious fuchsia and hydrangeas.
There were donkey rides for the children.

Sidmouth Apple Pudding

METHOD
Peel, core and chop the apples. Beat the egg and the
sugar together. The milk is then heated with the
breadcrumbs and cinnamon. As it heats up put in 1 oz
butter. Take off the fire and when it has cooled, add
the beaten egg and sugar and the apples. Butter a pie
dish and bake in a very moderate oven for an hour.

INGREDIENTS

½ lb apples
1 breakfast cup breadcrumbs
2 oz butter
A pinch of cinnamon
1 pint milk
1 egg
2 oz caster sugar

Top right: Connaught Gardens at Sidmouth in 1961.

Right: Sidmouth, East Devon.

Salcombe Devonshire Junket

METHOD

To the milk add the brandy and the sugar. Pour into a china dish with the rennet. When set, spread thick Devonshire cream over the top. Grate a little nutmeg over the cream and from the sugar caster sprinkle a little sparkling sugar.

INGREDIENTS

1 quart milk (warm)
1 tablespoon brandy
1 tablespoon sugar
2 teaspoons rennet
Devonshire cream
Nutmeg
Sparkling sugar

Salcombe has one of the West Country's best natural harbours, a favourite with yachtsmen and owners of small boats, which can find their way up the estuary as far as Kingsbridge. This small old town has a popular regatta, first held in 1857.

Salcombe, with one of the finest harbours in the West Country, is still a favourite haven of yachtsmen. Its first regatta was held in 1587. This card dates from 1905 and shows the Marine Hotel, then famous for its lobsters and seafood.

Damson Jam

METHOD
Simmer the washed, ripe damsons in the water until soft. Skim off stones as they surface. Stir in the sugar. Bring to boil and keep stirring until a set is reached. Pot straight away.

INGREDIENTS

4 lb damsons
4 lb sugar
½ pint water

The story of Hallsands, a fishing village of twenty cottages nestling under high red cliffs and protected by a shingle beach, shows how natural sea defences should never be removed.

In 1897, a contractor was allowed to take 650,000 tons of gravel and as a result, in spite of a sea wall, Hallsands was left open to fierce south-westerly gales. In 1917 a storm raged for four days, and so severely battered the cottages that only one was left fit to live in; a terrifying time for the villagers.

Sisters Ella and Patience Trout lost their home but later built a hotel on the cliffs and rescued an American seaman from a sinking ship.

Ashburton Victoria Sandwich

METHOD
Heat oven to 180° C. Place all ingredients in a bowl or electric mixer and beat well. Turn into 8-inch cake tin and bake for ½ hour. When cool, split and fill with the following jam.

INGREDIENTS

4 oz flour
4 oz butter
1 tablespoon water
4 oz caster sugar
2 eggs

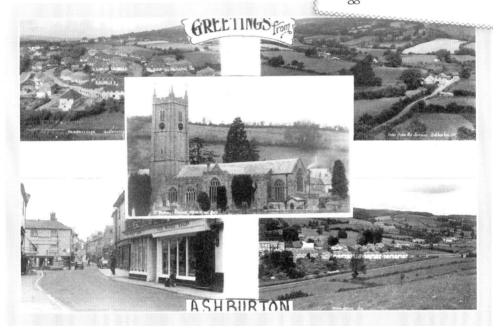

Old-fashioned Ashburton Raspberry Jam

METHOD
Place the fruit in a large basin over boiling water. Crush fruit with a wooden spoon. Add the hot sugar and stir until sugar is dissolved. Turn all into a preserving pan and boil for 10 minutes only. The lovely flavour of the raspberries is retained to perfection and together you have the perfect sponge cake. Queen Victoria was very fond of this cake, which was made countrywide in her reign. I have come across the same recipe in a number of regions.

INGREDIENTS

6 lb raspberries
6 lb preserving sugar

Barnstaple Chocolate Soufflé

METHOD
Melt the butter, add the flour and stir in the milk.
Melt the chocolate on top of a double saucepan.
Add the sugar and hot water and combine with
the sauce just made. Add the yolks of eggs, well
beaten, fold in the whites beaten until stiff and
dry. Flavour with vanilla and bake in a buttered
soufflé dish in a moderate oven at 150° C for 30–45
minutes. Serve the chocolate soufflé with a foamy
sauce made as follows:

METHOD
Cream the butter, add the flour and sugar
gradually, stirring constantly. Add the egg yolk,
well beaten, the water and the vanilla. Cook in a
double boiler until the mixture thickens, stirring
constantly. Cool, then add the stiffly beaten egg
white just before serving.

INGREDIENTS

1 oz butter
1 oz unsweetened grated
    chocolate
2 tablespoons hot water
½ teaspoon vanilla
½ oz flour
1 gill milk
2 oz sugar
3 eggs

THE SAUCE

1 oz butter
4 oz sugar
1 teaspoon vanilla
½ oz flour
1 gill water
1 egg

The Horse and Groom Inn in Barnstaple, we noticed as we walked past in October
1989, is now much enlarged. Another old inn is the Three Tuns. In 1850 there were
twenty-six beer houses and fifty-six inns and taverns. Barnstaple also had at that
time sixteen maltsters and twenty-three groceries and tea dealers. Names which
featured then are still around today: Bowden; Quick; Soper; Thorne. Said to be the
oldest borough in England, it still has the Tome Stone, resembling a sun dial, on
Georgian Queen Anne's Walk, where merchants and shipowners struck bargains.

Dating back from Saxon
times, Barnstaple is
one of four Devon
boroughs mentioned in
the Domesday Book of
1086. At Bideford and
Barnstaple are bridges
dating from the Middle
Ages. Every Friday, cream
and butter are sold in the
famous Pannier Market.
The Imperial Hotel and
the Albert Clock are
shown in this view of the
Square in the 1920s.

Stoke Abbott Steamed Raspberry Pudding

METHOD
Mix flour, jam and suet in a basin and bind with the egg and milk. Mix thoroughly. Grease a pudding basin and pour in the mixture. Place a circle of greaseproof paper on top and tie down firmly. Put in a steamer and cook for 2 hours on a low burner. Simple but delicious pudding.

INGREDIENTS

2 teacups self-raising flour
1 teacup raspberry jam or fresh raspberries
½ teacup chopped suet
1 egg

The former name of this village, which reached through high-hedged lanes bright with ragged robin and bluebells (intensely blue in spring), was Abbott Stock, when the monks lived there and dairy farming was their main occupation.

Dawlish Warren Devon Cream Biscuits

METHOD
Sift the flour into the clotted cream. Add the egg, working the mixture with the fingertips until it is like very fine crumbs. Add the sugar, setting aside 1 oz. Add a very little milk and roll out thinly this pastry-like mixture on a floured board. Cut into small rounds and sprinkle each with the remaining sugar. Place on a greased baking tray and bake at 200° C for 15 minutes.

INGREDIENTS

8 oz clotted cream
4 oz caster sugar
1½ tablespoons milk
1 lb plain flour
1 large beaten egg

Dawlish Warren, showing the railway station and beach. The traveller by train sees one of the finest coastal stretches in the country – red sandstone cliffs and tunnels alongside the sea.

Lee Moor Gooseberry and Banana Pudding

METHOD

Gently stew the gooseberries with 4 tablespoons water. Rub them through a sieve. Make ½ pint of custard and flavour it with the lemon rind. Lay the sponge fingers in a glass dish. Squeeze the juice from the lemon onto them and spread the gooseberry and honey pulp over them. Mash the bananas with a fork and put this on top. Pour the warm custard over this. Serve cold in summer but warm in winter.

INGREDIENTS

1 lb gooseberries (mellow type)
½ cup honey
½ lemon
½ pint custard
6 sponge fingers

Widdecombe-in-the-Moor Strawberry Pie

METHOD

Sift dry ingredients together, rub in butter very lightly with fingertips and add water slowly to make a stiff dough. Roll out on a floured board and use for bottom crust of pie, being careful to fold the paste well over the edge of the pie plate. Bake in a hot oven for 12–15 minutes. If glazed crust is desired, brush edges after baking with boiling hot syrup (2 tablespoons syrup and a tablespoon water) and return to oven for 1–2 minutes until syrup hardens. Fill the baked crust with fresh selected hulled strawberries and cover with syrup made as follows:

INGREDIENTS

1 cup float
2 teaspoons baking powder
¼ cup cold water
½ teaspoon salt
4 tablespoons butter
1 quart strawberries

Add ½ cup sugar and ½ cup strawberries to 2 cups boiling water. Bring to the boil and strain. Add 1 tablespoon corn starch, which has been mixed with a little cold water. Cook over a hot fire for a minute or two, stirring constantly. Remove from fire and beat hard. Return to slow fire, cook very gently until thick. Pour while hot over strawberries. Serve either hot or cold.

Widdecombe Fairings

METHOD

Warm the butter in a pan, then take off the fire and stir in flour, syrup and sugar. A flat toffee tin should be buttered and into this the mixture placed in small spoonfuls, leaving room to spread. Bake in a hot oven for 10 minutes. Remove from tin with a palette knife and curve them round the handle of a wooden spoon. If they are to be filled with Devonshire clotted cream they need to be curled tightly.

INGREDIENTS

2 oz flour
1 dessertspoon caster sugar
½ oz ground ginger (optional)
2 oz unsalted butter
2 oz syrup

The famous fair at Widdecombe may well be the oldest in England. Spiced ale was traditional besides fairings, a word which applied to a host of novelties, not merely the sweetmeat or the gingerbread stall. There were trays of neck and shoulder ribbons, tin lockets with glass stones. Over a century ago the merry-go-round was trundled full circle by two heavy horses. There was the panorama showing some historical event, the coconut shy, the fighting booth and the shooting gallery. At the general fairs Devonshire merchants 'offered serges, shalloons and kerseys'.

St Pancras church on Widdecombe-in-the-Moor is known as 'The Cathedral-in-the-Moor'. Appropriate to Old Devon Recipes is a 1932 postcard issued by F. W. Broughton of the Old Inn, Widdecombe-in-the-Moors, and also its subject, Widdecombe Green Tea Rooms. The homely 'teas' sign is one of hundreds, less homely today, but the ancient, thatched, granite cottages clustered round the green remain very attractive. The bowmen of Widdecombe used to practise archery after church on the 'butte park' or village green.

Woolacombe and Lustleigh Shortbread

METHOD
The oven should be heated to 180°C. Sift flour into the mixing bowl, setting aside the bran. Rub in the butter until the mixture resembles fine crumbs. Stir in the brown sugar. Knead the mixture into a dough, then flatten into round shape to fit into a buttered tin. Prick with a fork and just before putting in the oven, scatter the bran over the surface of the shortbread. Cook for 25 minutes.

INGREDIENTS

4 oz wholemeal flour
4 teaspoons brown sugar
3 oz unsalted butter

This is an old basic recipe for this ever-popular sweetmeat, also beloved of Queen Victoria, and which is only really delicious if made with butter.

The beach from the sandhills at Woolacombe around 1951. The Downs climb steeply from here, yellow with gorse most of the year. Nearby Barricane Beach is famous for its sea shells, which get swept ashore into this rocky cove. Morte Point is a favourite walk.

Woolacombe Sands. Woolacombe Down rises steeply above the sands and is popular for walkers. Others are drawn to the Barricane Beach, a cove noted for sea shells swept in by boisterous tides at Woolacombe.

Totnes Chocolate Cake

METHOD

Melt the chocolate in a bowl set over simmering water. Whip egg whites and caster sugar until stiff. Fold in the chocolate, then the whipped cream. Chill. Cut the sponge cake into 3 equal parts. Moisten 2 sections with the sugar syrup. Line a 9-inch cake tin with half of the remaining cake and cover this with the whipped chocolate mixture. Repeat with the second part of the cake. Chill and leave to set.

   Grated dark chocolate, if desired, can be scattered on top of the cake but we found it rich enough with the mousse filling.

INGREDIENTS

4 egg whites
4 oz caster sugar
4 oz dark chocolate
¾ pint whipped Devon cream
¼ pint sugar syrup
1 Victoria sponge cake
1 tall-sided cake tin with removable base

The river at Totnes, 1950. Exports of tin and wool made the ancient town prosperous from the Middle Ages and ships with Russian timber still sail up the River Dart, unloading at St Peter's Quay. The three-arched bridge shown in this beautiful study by Judges Ltd was built in 1828 to replace a thirteenth-century one, the remains of which still show at low tide.

This original watercolour by David Skipp shows one of Totnes' most notably interesting buildings: the East Gate, bridging the High Street, dating from the early sixteenth century. There are other very eye-catching architectural gems from the days of 'good Queen Bess' in Totnes.

Buckfast Honey Muesli

METHOD

Peel and cut the apples, sprinkling them with a little lemon juice. Peel and chop bananas, grapes, apricots or any other fruit. Cover the oatmeal with milk and honey and leave for 1 hour, topping up with milk as it soaks in. Store this mixture in the refrigerator. Half an hour before serving bring to room temperature to get the best flavour. Stir all gently.

We had this daily to set us up for recipe hunting and favoured using Devonshire double cream instead of milk. (Courtesy Mr Maurice Hanssen)

INGREDIENTS

4 eating apples
2 ripe bananas
2–4 tablespoons honey
Sultanas, grapes, peaches optional
4 cups of oatmeal
Lemon juice and milk

The monks at Buckfast Abbey worked in masonry and stained glass, tended bees and produced mead and abbey-brewed Buckfast tonic wine. In January 1907, six monks commenced the building of the magnificent Abbey church, finally completed in 1937. The monastery was founded in 1018 but at the Dissolution of the Monasteries the monks were forced to leave and the buildings fell into ruin.

It is reported by Maurince Hanssen, in his selection of wholesome recipes incorporating honey, that their honey has been produced since well before the Reformation. Brother Adam still looks after the Apiary at the age of ninety. In a good year many tons of aromatic Dartmoor honey could be collected.

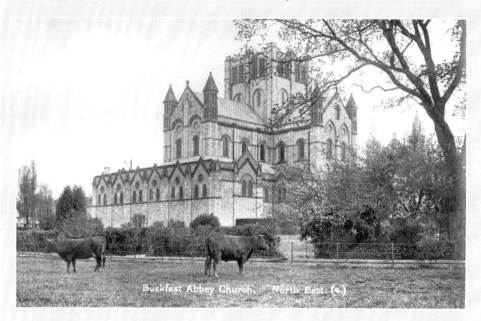

Buckfast Abbey Church. North East. (4)

Cockington Date and Walnut Loaf

METHOD

Mix together all these with a pinch of salt (optional). Steep the dates in milk, then drain off excess liquid. Add to the mixture 2 oz melted margarine or butter, 2 beaten eggs and a little milk. Bake in a moderate oven for 1 hour. This makes 3 loaves. (Courtesy Mrs Barbara Strachan)

INGREDIENTS

12 oz cut-up dates
1 lb self-raising flour
2 oz chopped walnuts
12 oz sugar
A small quantity of milk

Cockington Forge remains part of the village's rural simplicity and picturesque style, which have made it a favourite subject for artists. The blacksmith is examining each hoof of the horse in this postcard from 1947. In the 1890s it was possible to hire a pony and trap, and approach these lovely thatched cottages through leafy Devonshire lanes, passing Tor Abbey and the hamlet of Chelston. Sensibly preserved as a tourist attraction, horse-drawn carriages still transport visitors to Cockington. The fifteenth-century red-sandstone church is perfect in that setting, and the modern Druin Inn, designed by Sir Edwin Lutyens in 1934, has a thatched roof and long chimney pots. The smithy dates from the fourteenth century.

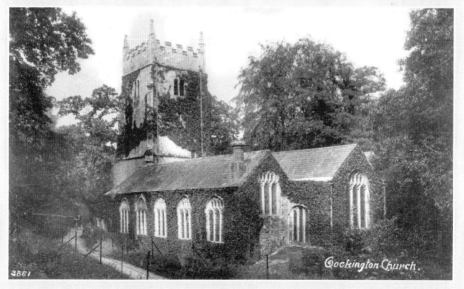

Crediton Pan Cake

METHOD
Beat the milk and egg together and mix well. Mix
the flour, salt, butter and lard well then add the egg
and milk. Finally stir in the dried fruits. Roll out on
a floured board, making it the size of the base of the
pan bottom and put the cake upon it. Cook slowly so
that the cake browns top and bottom. It can be more
conveniently cooked in the oven on moderate heat
for 1 hour. Then split open with a warmed, sharp
carving knife and spread with butter.

INGREDIENTS

½ lb sultanas and
    currants
1 egg
4 oz butter
Pinch of salt
½ pint milk
11 oz flour
2 oz dripping or lard

Clovelly Gooseberry Pudding

METHOD
Mix suet and flour together. Add the sugar, washed,
topped and tailed gooseberries, mixing all well
together. Put into a well-buttered basin which should
be tied down with a cloth and boiled for 3 hours.
Traditionally this eighteenth-century pudding was
eaten with more sugar, but an egg custard sauce
makes a good accompaniment.

INGREDIENTS

4 oz grated suet
6 oz gooseberries
8 oz flour
4 oz brown sugar

Clovelly, the perfect seaside village owes much of its
protection to Christine Hamlyn, who owned the estate
from 1834 to 1936 Her preservation of unique beauty
along steep High Street (known as 'Up-along and
Down-along'), paved with pebbles from the beach,
has Tudor cottages bearing her initials. The best way
to Clovelly is along Hobby Drive, running through
woodland. Still a toll road, it was built by Sir James
Hamlyn Williams.

'Mending the nets', Clovelly, also shows lobster pots
another source of harvest from the sea. The most
picturesque approach is the three-mile-long Hobby Drive
running through Woodlands. 'Had duck and greenpeas
and came back on the mail coach' is written on this 1905
postcard in July of that year.

More examples of 'Devon thatch' and spring cherry blossom in J. Salmon's photograph of cottages at North Bovey, Dartmoor. (Courtesy J. Salmon, Sevenoaks)

Devonshire Clotted Cream

Nothing on earth, or in poet's dream
Is so rich and rare as Devonshire cream

METHOD

In a wide bowl, place fresh, not pasteurised milk. Leave it to stand. In summertime this took 10 hours, in winter 24 hours. The bowl is then placed on low heat. As in Cornwall it could be the slab of an old coal-fired cooking range. Very gradually it needs to be warmed to below boiling point and this temperature maintained but the milk should never boil. On top of the milk a thick crust forms then leave the bowl to cool until next day, when the clotted (old Devonshire word is 'clouted') cream is ready to be skimmed off. One elderly Devon cowherd believed that the red cattle of old produced the richest cream but had not the high milk yield of the well-known Friesian breed which replaced them.

Views of Bigbury-on-Sea overlooking Burgh Island. Cottages at Ringmore near to Bigbury-on-Sea with roofs of Devon thatch lend a distinctly old world charm. Burgh Island is linked only at low tide to the mainland. It has a fourteenth-century inn romantically linked with smugglers and from there the bay used to be anxiously scanned for pilchards before their shoals reclined.

Devon Drinks, Jam and Toffee

Oddicombe Toffee Apples

METHOD
Melt the butter. Add the treacle and sugar and stir gently till it boils. In 15 minutes when a spoonful is dropped in water, it hardens. Allow it to cool a little. Wash and wipe apples, removing any stalks, and stick a wooden skewer in each. Dip in the thickened toffee and place upright in a jar on a plate, allowing toffee apple to set.

INGREDIENTS

1 lb small eating apples
4 oz butter
6–8 sharpened wooden skewers (from butchers)
1 lb treacle
1 lb demerara sugar

Oddicombe Beach, a fine sandy beach at the foot of Babbacombe Downs, was completely secluded from the busy world in 1900. It was one of the three beaches in the area where mixed bathing was allowed. A tiny refreshment hut can be seen dwarfed by high cliffs from where strawberries and cream, jugs of tea and thickly buttered scones could be bought.

Woolacombe Barley Water

METHOD
Boil half a cupful of pearl barley in one cup full of cold water. Let it simmer gently for half an hour. Pare the rind thinly off a large, fresh lemon and place in a jug. Strain the barley water into the jug and let it infuse for 10 minutes with the jug covered, when it will be ready for drinking.

This nineteenth-century cooling drink was welcome at hay-making time and was reputedly known to alleviate backache.

Treacle Posset

METHOD

Another old remedy thought to be good for colds was made by stirring a teaspoon of black treacle into a cupful of warm milk. Alternatively, a teaspoon of honey stirred into warm milk was soothing to sore throats and we considered not only good for getting an excitable child off to sleep but it also served as a gentle, acceptable aperient, as did the treacle posset.

1910 Cadbury's Cocoa advertisement. Cocoa drinks for a large family were made in a samovar, and cocoa powder was used in some chocolate cakes.

Widdecombe-in-the-Moor Rose-hip Purée

METHOD

Wash and trim the hips. Cut in half and scoop out the seeds with a salt spoon. Boil in water. Cover the fruit and stir until it becomes tender. Put through a blender. Add lemon juice and sugar to taste. Serve this concentrated purée with roast meat.

Many gardens now have *Rosa rugosa* hedges smothered in flowers during summer, which convert to rose-hips in the autumn. Gathered, these will make a purée rich in vitamin C.

INGREDIENTS

2 ¼ lb rose-hips
4 cups water
Juice of 1 large lemon
Sugar

Rose-hip Jelly

METHOD
Cut hips in half and scoop out seeds with a salt spoon.
Boil fruit in water until a setting point is reached. A
small quantity can be tested on a cold saucer. Gently
stroke the jelly. It will wrinkle if setting point has been
reached. Beware of overcooking.

INGREDIENTS

4 cups of ripe rose-hips
2 cups water
2 cups sugar

Mother's Hedgerow Jam was always a winner, made from rose-hips, sloes,
blackberries, wild strawberries. Her Wild Blackberry Pie she made by first cooking
the blackberries (which are usually very 'seedy') and straining the juice from them
on to gently cooked apple, a union which resulted in splendid fruit filling, without
the crunchiness of seeds which can be excruciating when they wander under dental
plates. However, she never made wine, classing it with 'strong drink' which she
would not touch, having signed the Temperance Pledge when she was sixteen.

Hedgerow Wine

This recipe from Buckfast has an ecclesiastical source and must surely have been
made since wild blackberries bloomed in early autumn and the fruits of the forest
were noticed by hungry natives.

METHOD
Wash the fruit, then pour the boiling water over it.
Leave for one week. Each day mash the fruit with a
wooden spoon. Strain and squeeze all the liquid from
the fruit. Strain through muslin and add the sugar,
stirring until quite dissolved. The yeast should then
be spread upon the toast and floated on the wine
which can then be placed in a warm area to ferment.
After a week it can be skimmed and bottled.

INGREDIENTS

1 gallon wild blackberries
1 gallon boiling water
½ oz yeast
2 lb sloes
8 oz sugar
1 slice of toast

Instead of the cold tea served to most agricultural workers at harvest time, home-
brewed herb beer was provided for field and forest workers as it was found that the
men worked better off this. I was interested to hear about the old custom of sealing a
bargain with a mug of ale.

Lynmouth Blackcurrant Fool

METHOD

Cook the blackcurrants with 3 oz sugar until soft, simmering gently. Put the milk on to heat, taking sufficient to mix the custard powder and the remaining sugar to a smooth cream. Add to the milk when nearly boiling and stir for a few minutes. Strain the blackcurrants, saving the juice and sieving the fruit. Stir the fruit purée into the custard when the latter is quite cold, adding the cream and some of the blackcurrant juice to achieve a nice consistency. Put into individual glasses and serve chilled with thick cream or yoghurt.

INGREDIENTS

1 lb blackcurrants
¾ pint full cream milk
2 tablespoons custard powder
4 oz caster sugar
¼ pint cream

Lynton, high on a cliff-top 600 feet above Lynmouth, became fashionable at the time of the Napoleonic Wars. The resort was known for its water-powered cliff railway and a fine town hall, built by the publisher Geroge Newnes. Countisbury Common, in the area, is on the North Devon Coastal Path.

Lynmouth, originally a fishing village, was developed in the Victorian times but became world news when in 1952 it was devastated by great floods. The River Lyn burst its banks and swept away many houses at night-time when villagers were abed, drowning thirty-four people.

Countisbury Hill backs Lynmouth, whose oldest area is Mars Hill. The author of *Lorna Doone*, Richard Doddridge Blackmore, stayed at Lynmouth when he was writing his famous novel.

At County Gate the road crosses the Somerset–Devon boundary and can take walkers to Glenthorne, part of a 3-mile nature trail. Sillery Sands and Watersmeet, even Countisbury Common are accessible, cliffs on the Western side of the Common rise over 900 feet, the highest in England. Usually hiked from Lynmouth, this 1961 card shows Mars Hill and the Rising Sun Hotel (right), well known for good food.

A Judges Ltd view shows two paddle steamers off Lynmouth in the early 1900s.

On Dartmoor are Bronze Age remains and it is written of this bleak moorland that 'nowhere in Britain has a greater density of prehistoric remains and nowhere in Britain can you feel the same brooding sense of a past extending over 5000 years.' Combstone was, for us, one of the most impressive of Dartmoor's granite outcrops.

Hundreds of feet above the sea is the panoramic coast road running from Lynton to Porlock. It is one of the finest for its views of sea, sky and moorland, dominated by Dunkery Beacon at 1,708 feet high. Here you may see groups of wild ponies but out of sight are the wooded, deep coombes, haunt of wild red deer.

It is still unspoilt as it was when R. D. Blackmore, 130 years ago, wrote his romantic novel *Lorna Doone*. You may see ancient monoliths or a disused iron mine but the fierce Doones have long disappeared. After Blackmore's death in 1900 there were more attempts to authenticate their existence.

Dartmoor ponies were first mentioned in the will of a Saxon bishop from Crediton. Wild and shaggy-maned, the public are warned not to feed these ponies, which have grazed on Dartmoor since the Dark Ages. They are rounded up and branded every autumn.

Gooseberry Fool

METHOD
Simmer the fruit and sugar with a little water in a stainless steel pan. Put the fruit mixture in a blender and turn it into a purée. Whisk the double cream until stiff then fold in the cold purée. Looks nicest in individual glasses with a star of cream piped on after chilling for about an hour.

INGREDIENTS

1 lb gooseberries, washed, topped, tailed
½ pint double cream
4 oz sugar

Treacle Toffee Caramel

METHOD
Melt sugar and butter in a pan. Add treacle. Bring to boil. Add the milk slowly and stir all the time. Test for set. Pour into a square, well buttered tin and mark into sections as it cools.

INGREDIENTS

6 oz sugar
1 small tin evaporated milk
8 oz treacle
6 oz unsalted butter

Photographed in the 1890s, this was the type of bathing machine wheeled around the sea. in the very early days swimming costumes were voluminous or not worn at all. Revd F Kievent complained bitterly about wearing 'drawers'. 'The rough waves tore them down to my ankles.' Nudity was tolerated at some beaches reserved for men but there was also censure. In 1895 there were four bathing places for men and four for ladies. Byelaws required proprietors of machines to supply 'costume and two towels for six pence an hour'.

Treacle Toffee

METHOD
Dissolve sugar in water. Add treacle and butter. Boil up to 150° C. Stir gently. Shield for spattering, using pan lid. Add lemon juice, then pour into well-buttered tin. As the treacle toffee cools mark it into small squares with a knife. When it is cold, wrap pieces in greaseproof paper twists and store in a cake tin with a well-fitting lid.

INGREDIENTS

1 lb demerara sugar
2 oz butter
Juice of 1 lemon
6 oz treacle
1 pint water

Butterscotch

METHOD

Melt butter in a strong saucepan. Add sugar, syrup and water. Bring to boil, adding almond and cream of tartar. Stir all the time for 10 minutes. To test to see if toffee is ready, drop a small quantity into iced water. It should form into a firm, hard ball. Pour into well-buttered tin. Mark into squares as it cools. When really firm, break into small sections and wrap each in greaseproof paper. Store in an airtight tin.

INGREDIENTS

½ lb light golden syrup
1 lb caster sugar
Pinch of cream of tartar
¼ lb unsalted butter
1 teaspoon almond essence
1 tablespoon cold water

Torbay Mint and Apple Chutney (Pound Chutney)

METHOD

Wash apples. Core them and chop finely. Mince the mint leaves and onions. Slice the washed tomatoes and mix all together in a large, stainless steel pan with the other ingredients. Stir until the sugar is dissolved then, from time to time, as the chutney simmers and softens for 45 minutes. The ginger root should then be removed and the chutney potted in warm jars and labelled. We found the chutney from this recipe useful up to and beyond Christmas, especially after a poor summer had left a harvest of green tomatoes.

INGREDIENTS

1 lb cooking apples
1 lb sultanas
1 lb sugar
1 pint malt vinegar
1 lb onions
1 lb green tomatoes
1 oz ginger root
1 bunch fresh mint

The *Flying Scotsman* locomotive on a Torbay Steam Railway service (Paignton–Kingswear) passed Goodrington in our summer stay in 1973. A name of enduring fame, in that year the *Flying Scotsman* had come back from the United States and made a great impression in the Torquay area on visitors and steam enthusiasts. *Railway World* recalled when an engine driver seeing two people on Goodrington Sands station platform called out, 'Do you want the train?' 'Yes!' He quickly stopped to avoid overrunning the platform!

The *Flying Scotsman*.

Axminster Blackberry Wine

METHOD

Wash and pick the fruit (elderberries may be used instead of blackberries). Boil the water and pour over the fruit. Allow to cool. Add yeast. Cover and leave for a week, when it should be strained and the sugar added. Stir sugar in till all dissolved, then add the raisins. Cover and leave to work for a further week. Bottle when all fermentation has ceased. It is ready for drinking in 6 months.

INGREDIENTS

4 quarts ripe blackberries
1¼ teaspoons fresh yeast
7 lb sugar
5 quarts water
1 lb raisins

The blackberries should be just ripe and gathered on a dry day. Use a vessel with a tap fitted at the bottom. Put the fruit in this and cover with boiling water. After it has cooled, mash the berries with both hands and then let them stand covered for 4 days. Draw off the liquid into another vessel. Now, to every gallon allow 1 lb sugar, mixing well. Put it into a cask to work for 10 days, keeping the cask well filled and discarding the lees of the liquid. When it has ceased to work bung it down. In 6 months the wine may be bottled.

Axminster Raspberry Wine

METHOD

3 lb raisins should be washed, stoned and cleaned thoroughly. Boil 2 gallons of spring water for ½ hour. Pour this boiling water over the raisins in a deep, stone jar. Add 6 quarts of fresh raspberries and 2 lb loaf sugar. Stir well and place in a cool larder. Cover. Stir it twice a day, then pass through a hair sieve, next day adding 1 lb more of sugar. Put into a barrel and when fine, in about 2 months, it can be bottled.

INGREDIENTS

3 lb raisins
2 gallons water
6 quarts raspberries
3 lb loaf sugar

Spiced Ale

METHOD

Heat slowly but do not allow to boil. Add all ingredients except apple. Take off the heat and keep warm by the fire for 15 minutes. Strain and put the apple slices in a punch bowl with ladle.

INGREDIENTS

4 pints ale
2 sliced Cox's apples
Pinch of nutmeg
2 teaspoons sugar
Pinch of spice
3 whole cloves

Barnstaple Fair dates from the Middle Ages.
Its opening takes place at the Guildhall, when spiced ale, brewed
from a closely guarded Elizabethan recipe, is ladled into silver cups. All present
drink success to the fair. Above their heads hangs a large, white glove, the ancient
symbol which used to show outsiders that they could enter the fair and trade
freely in the town.

" Christ Jesus came into the world to save sinners."
I Tim. 1, 15.

Barnstaple Town Station. Lynton and Barnstaple Railway.

Frumenty

Sold at the fairs, Frumenty was made from crushed whole wheat, sugar, allspice, raisins and skimmed milk, simmered in an earthenware pot in the fire oven overnight. Another popular fairing.

At the fair in Thomas Hardy's *The Mayor of Casterbridge*, amongst other distinctive country rustics was a homely character, the 'frumenty woman', who sold among the gingerbreads and other fairings a very popular dish called Frumenty. Everybody knew about it in the eighteenth and nineteenth centuries.

As I have been searching old recipes for years and was eagerly awaiting the first copies of *Traditional Yorkshire Recipes* off the press, I was thrilled to be presented with a large, yellowing envelope of relevant information, cuttings, 'receipts' and old photographs. Setting aside hot pot, throdkin, potato cakes, oatmeal pastry, brewis, lobscouse, praty cake and cowheel pie, I eagerly seized on the details of frument or frumenty, having heard quite a lot about this country favourite, but never before seen a receipt.

My grandfather used to enjoy it in the upland village of Belthorn in Lancashire and was one who disputed that 'only Yorkshire men knew what frumenty was'.

'When I was young,' he said, 'frumenty was looked on as a diet for the young or invalid and it bred some bonny Lancashire lads and lasses.' Possibly because it was associated with special occasions, like pancakes on Shrove Tuesday, it was eaten with great relish.

A Lincolnshire lady reported that it was very popular for its sustaining qualities at Harvest time and that it was eaten by the farm workers. 'It was made by the farmers' wives in the 1880s, as I remember, and given to the men at "clipping time" when the sheep shearing was being carried on and for the annual harvest supper, but as a special treat a cupful of rum was added.'

The custom of eating 'furmenty' in Devon was recalled by Mr T. H. Tomlinson of Otterton: 'I, along with the other boys, used to visit the farm houses and request wheat to make Furm a Tree, as we lads called it. The farmers, when wheat was being threshed, allowed the poor people of the villages to fetch a bowlful of wheat, fresh from the threshing machine, to make it for their families.' The same practice prevailed in Cumberland.

Devon Cream Toffee

METHOD

Melt 1 lb crushed sugar into ¼ lb butter. When nearly melted add by degrees ½ pint cream, stirring all the time. Boil until it is so thick you can hardly turn the spoon. Turn it into a tin which has been buttered. Smooth it with a clean knife. In a few minutes it will be ready to cut into squares. Quarter of an hour is usually long enough to boil it, but be careful for it easily burns. Stir without ceasing. Add ¼ teaspoon vanilla just before it is finished.

INGREDIENTS

1 lb crushed sugar
¼ lb butter
½ pint cream
¼ teaspoon vanilla

Buckfastleigh Chocolate Brandy

METHOD

Heat the chocolate and butter in a bowl over a saucepan of hot water until melted. Stir in the brandy and egg yolks. Add icing sugar and the trifle sponge rubbed down into crumbs. Leave for 30 minutes at bottom of fridge. Form the mixture into about 30 balls and roll them in the drinking chocolate.

INGREDIENTS

6 oz plain chocolate
2 dessertspoons brandy
2 oz icing sugar
2 oz trifle sponge
2 oz butter
2 egg yolks
2 tablespoons drinking chocolate

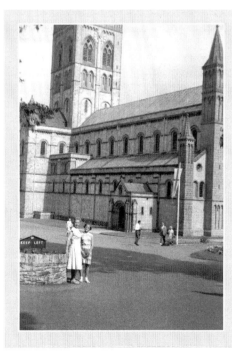

Mrs Dora Ware and daughter Barbara outside Buckfast Abbey, 1959.

Chudleigh Coconut Candy

METHOD
Mix the sugar and honey in a saucepan with the milk.
Boil for 15 minutes. Add the coconut and remove
from heat. Stir well for 2 minutes. Pour into wet tin.
When cold, cut into bars.

INGREDIENTS

2 oz honey
3 oz dessicated coconut
1 fl. oz milk
12 oz sugar
3 fl. oz water

Ilfracombe Hazelnut Butter

METHOD
Cream the butter and sugar. Add the essence and
beat in the chopped nuts. This makes a good sweet
sandwich spread.

INGREDIENTS

4 oz unsalted butter
4 oz chopped hazelnuts
   (cashew nuts or
   walnuts can be used
   instead)
4 oz caster sugar
½ teaspoon vanilla
   essence

A scene from 1928. Ilfracombe
was once the largest seaside
resort of North Devon, made
possible by the coming of the
railway. One of the few safe
havens on this coast, the harbour
is below Lantern Hill where the
Chapel of St Nicholas shows a
guiding light for sailors. White
Pebble Bay and Broadstrand,
with its delightful rock pools, are
favourites for children. The pool
is fresh with every tide.

Cherry Fruit Sauce

INGREDIENTS

1 large tin of fruit
½ pint juice
1 large orange
Butter
Water
2 teaspoons arrowroot
Glacé cherries

METHOD
From a large tin of fruit take about half a pint of juice
and add the juice of a large orange, making up with
water if necessary to ¾ pint. Add a nut of butter and
put juice on to heat. With a little cold water mix 2
level teaspoons of arrowroot to a smooth pasta and
stir into juice. Boil the syrup for 2 minutes until it
thickens. Add chopped glacé cherries to the sauce.

Apricot Sauce

METHOD

A quick way and a delicious sauce. Purée a can of apricots with their juice. Thin further with a tablespoon of rum and gently heat. For use with fritters.

INGREDIENTS

1 can of apricots
1 tablespoon rum

Okehampton Rough Cider

METHOD

Place the washed apples in a wooden tub and crush them. Pour the boiling water over them, cover with a scalded cloth and leave for a fortnight. Daily mash up the apples. After the fortnight strain off liquor and put in the bruised ginger root and ½ lb sugar to every pint of cider. Add a little extra boiling water. Stir well and put in the lemon juice and the halved lemon cases. Leave for another 2 weeks. Skim off any scum. Remove the lemon halves and ginger root and bottle lightly for 3 days, after which the tops can be firmly fixed and the cider left for 2 months before drinking. Another untested recipe, but we were warned of its potency. In the past, abuse of cider led to many a fight amongst labourers and seamen, but the number of apple recipes in this little book alone shows how fond the Devon people are of the cause of Adam and Eve's downfall.

INGREDIENTS

8 lb apples
4 lemons
2 gallons boiling water
8 lb sugar
1 fair-sized piece ginger root

On Twelfth Night, cider was poured onto the roots of the apple trees and wassailing commenced. 'Here's to the old apple tree etc. Hats full, caps full, bushel sacks full.'

At Ottery St Mary, as in other Devonshire towns, on 5 November flaming tar barrels were rolled down the street. In Victorian times these revels, connected with Guy Fawkes Night, often got out of hand, resulting in injury and much destruction to property. Hatherleigh did likewise on 5 November just before daybreak and at nightfall when a torchlight procession was held. Almost certainly these rituals would originate in the Celtic fire-raising ceremony called Samain. Treacle toffee, Devon butter toffee or gingerbread eating seem a much better idea these days...

Toffy

This toffee recipe is eighty years old and was simply called 'Toffy'.

METHOD
Take 3 lb of the best brown sugar and boil with 1½ pints of water until the candy hardens in cold water. Then add ½ lb of sweet flavoured fresh butter which will soften the toffy. Boil a few minutes until it again hardens and pour it into trays. It may be flavoured with lemon.

INGREDIENTS

3 lb brown sugar
1½ pints water
½ lb sweet flavoured butter
Lemon

An equally old recipe makes 'plot treacle toffy' from 1 lb white sugar, 1 cup treacle, ½ cup water, 1 teaspoon cream of tartar, boiling slowly. After boiling for 20 minutes, try it by dropping some in cold water. If it 'snaps' it is done. Pour into buttered tin dishes.

Kingsbridge Apple and Blackberry Jam

METHOD
Use good, sound fruit. Peel, core and cut the apples into small pieces. Add the water and simmer for 15 minutes. Crush the blackberries. Measure 1 lb prepared apples and juice into a preserving pan and mix with the prepared blackberries. Add the sugar and lemon juice. Heat slowly, stirring continuously until the sugar has dissolved. Add a small knob of butter and bring to a full rolling boil, stirring occasionally. Boil until a set is achieved.

INGREDIENTS

1 lb blackberries
1½ lb apples
¼ pint water
2 lb sugar
1 lemon

Kingsbridge had an active coastal trade in the nineteenth century with a ship-building yard and cattle market. The Market Arcade was restored in 1796. Lavish hospitality at Kingsbridge was noted, especially the brewing of 'White Ale', made from an old German recipe and said to be made on Saturday and tapped on Sunday! This is Hope Cove near Kingsbridge in 1938.

Kingsbridge Rowan Jelly

METHOD
Wash the berries and remove the stalks. Wash and cut up the apples but do not core or peel. In separate pans cover the fruits with cold water. Stew until the apples are soft and colour has flowed deeply red from the rowanberries. Drain off the juices without pressing the fruits. Measure the combined juices, allowing 1 lb sugar to every pint. Boil until a set is achieved, testing as you go to avoid over-boiling, which could produce a stiff jelly.

INGREDIENTS

3 lb rowanberries
1 lb sugar to each pint of juice
3 lb cooking apples

Dawlish Gooseberry and Elderflower Cream

METHOD
Rinse the gooseberries well, but there is no need to top and tail. Cook the gooseberries with the sugar over low heat for about 7 minutes. Add the elderflowers, washed. Stir well, leave for 5 minutes then take out the 4 heads of flowers. Sieve the fruit into a bowl and leave until cold, when you can fold in the stiffly whipped cream (do not over-whip it). Leave covered on a cold, marble slab until ready to dish up.

INGREDIENTS

1 lb gooseberries
4 heads elderflowers
4 oz fine sugar
¼ pint double Devonshire cream

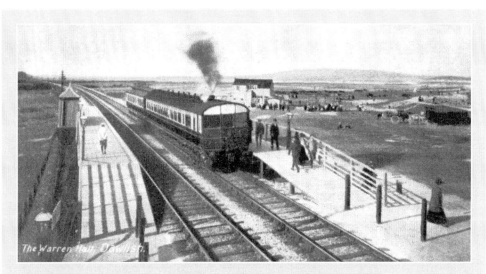

The Warren Halt at Dawlish around 1902. Later known as Dawlish Warren.

Brannoc, a sixteenth-century Devon saint, taught the people of Braunton to till the soil and rear cattle. It was said he used wild deer to pull the plough. When someone stole his cow and put it in the cooking pot, St Brannoc called it forth. Whole again, it continued to supply him with milk for a long time after this event.

Rockford Tomato Chutney

METHOD

Pour boiling water over the tomatoes to split the skins. Peel and cut up tomatoes, apples, onion and stir in other ingredients. Boil for 2 hours in a well-sealed kitchen, otherwise the scent of vinegar permeates the house. Pack into sterilised bottles, seal and label.

Honey can be used to glaze game, chicken and lamb cutlets, and to take the place of sugar in desserts and puddings. Indeed, stewed fruits are vastly improved by honey rather than by adding sugar. Grilled, honeyed grapefruit, uncooked strawberries, blackberries or raspberries, dribbled with honey, all make quick, easy and beneficial sweets.

INGREDIENTS

4 lb tomatoes
2 lb sultanas
1 lb clover honey
½ cup malt vinegar
1 teaspoon salt
1 lb apples
1 large onion
Juice of 2 lemons
½ teaspoon crushed cloves
½ lb dates washed and pre-soaked in water

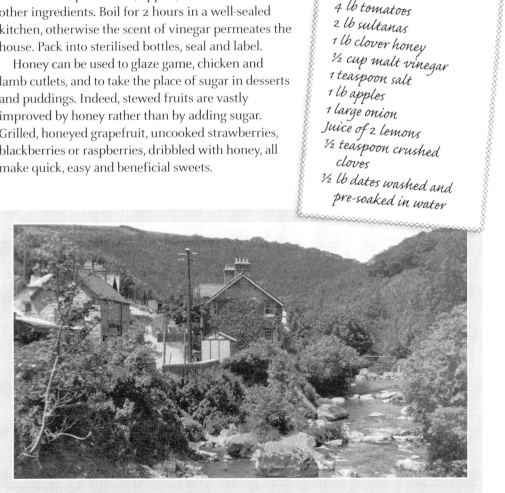

Rockford. (Courtesy Judges Ltd)

Babbacombe Greengage Fool

METHOD
Put the cleaned greengages in a pan with the sugar
and 2 tablespoons of water and stew gently. Rub
this through a sieve. Crack 4 of the greengage
kernels. Crack and chop these up finely. Add to the
greengage. Whip the cream until stiff and mix with
the purée. Fill a bowl or individual glasses and allow
to set. Serve with cream or custard.

INGREDIENTS

1 lb ripe greengages
¼ lb pounded sugar
1 gill cream
2 tablespoons water

    Apricots could be used instead. This apricot
filling is excellent as sandwich in a butter sponge cake: Combine 1 cup of
thick apricot sauce made by stewing sweetened, strained apricots flavoured with a
little brandy and 1 cup of clotted cream, whipped.

Thought to be one of the oldest inhabited sites discovered in Britain, Kent's Cavern on the Babbacombe
road was explored in the nineteenth century revealing the bones of cave bears, cave lions and sabre-
toothed tigers, remains going back 30,000 years. Today's visitors find the cavern well lit but early visitors
to Phillip's stalactite and bone cavern used candles. The dripping limestone formed remarkable stalactites.